£ 2.49

MARIA MARTEN

MARIA MARTEN
THE MURDER IN THE RED BARN

PETER HAINING

AN
IMAGES
PUBLICATION

MARIA MARTEN - THE MURDER IN THE RED BARN © 1992
RICHARD CASTELL PUBLISHING LIMITED

A revised and redesigned edition of
BURIED PASSIONS
first published in Great Britain in 1980 by
Neville Spearman Limited

© Peter Haining 1980 & 1992

ISBN 0 948134 31 3

Designed and typeset by Castell Design & Print, Plymouth

Printed by The Cromwell Press
Broughton Gifford, Melksham, Wiltshire

Published in Great Britain by Richard Castell Publishing Limited
24 Queens Road, Lipson, Plymouth PL4 7PL

an IMAGES publication

For

My family
Philippa, Richard, Sean & Gemma,
and all our friends in Boxford, Suffolk.

ACKNOWLEDGEMENTS

I should like to express my thanks to a number of individuals and organisations who helped me during the writing of this book. Firstly, David Philips for loaning me rare books about the Red Barn murder; John Mead and Joe Chamberlaine who took the photographs of Polstead as it is today; and Philip Streeting for the map of the district. Also the staffs at the British Museum and the London Library; Moyse's Hall Museum, Bury St. Edmunds, Suffolk; The British Film Institute; Bruton Photography for copying many of the rare prints which appear in the book; The Estate of R. Thurston Hopkins and Samuel French Ltd. My thanks also to *The Guardian, The Sunday Times, East Anglian Daily Times* and the *Evening Gazette,* Colchester, for allowing me to quote from their newspapers. Especial thanks to Mrs. Elizabeth Poole for typing the manuscript, and all the good people of Polstead who helped me with their reminiscences of the story which has made their delightful little village famous all over the world. And, finally, to all those who have asked for this book to be brought back into print and Mel Birch who has made it happen.

Peter Haining 1992

ABOUT THE AUTHOR - Peter Haining developed his investigative skills during his years as a successful journalist and has published over fifty books based on a wide variety of subjects, translated into twelve languages. Famous names which have come under his scrutiny include Charlie Chaplin, David Niven, Brigitte Bardot, Greta Garbo, Raquel Welch and

several books on Elvis Presley. He has also published international bestsellers about the highly popular TV series on Sherlock Holmes and Doctor Who.

Among the list of diverse subjects into which he has delved are the supernatural, bullfighting, natural phenomena and ballooning.

Peter, who is 52, lives with his family at Boxford, a peaceful village in the heart of the Suffolk countryside.

CONTENTS

Idyllic Polstead - the setting of one of the most famous crimes in history. The home of William Corder faces over the village pond.

INTRODUCTION
The Ghost of William Corder

* * *

I T HAD BEEN a typical May day in Suffolk - the last chill of winter that was still in the air warmed away by a glorious sun that promised a hot summer. The little village of Polstead had basked in this uninterrupted sunshine all morning and through the long afternoon: the only signs of activity being a pair of anglers who had sat patiently beside a pond and the occasional villager passing up and down the sloping main street between the small, pink-washed houses, some stopping to pass the time of day as they went about their business.

As evening started to fall, those who first experienced what has since become an almost regular haunting, remembered that a sudden, rather strange silence fell over the village. Few, though, back in those middle years of the 1920s, appreciated the significance of the day in question until some time later - when the ghost that walked through Polstead became a topic of conversation, not to mention controversy.

There were already shadows around the beamed facade of what is known as "Corder's House" perched on its hill overlooking the pond, when a strange-looking figure was seen to glide across the garden. A figure dressed in what appeared to be a Victorian frock coat and hat. Those who saw the ghost recall that although the figure was indistinct, it gave every indication of being a man intent on a mission of some kind. Moments later, they said, the figure had disappeared as suddenly and mysteriously as it had appeared. What those folk - and everyone else who has subsequently seen the figure - is in no doubt about is that the phantom was moving quite deliberately away from the house towards the *east*.

This curious phenomenon has, in fact, been repeated in Polstead in the intervening years on several occasions - mostly when the date May 18 falls on a Friday, for this is the anniversary of one of the best known and most curious murders in history. For on that spring day in the year 1827

11

William Corder, who lived in the farmhouse that still bears his name, slipped away to meet the pretty young village girl he had made pregnant and was apparently intending to take to Ipswich to marry, but instead - so the legend goes - brutally murdered her and buried her body in the red-tiled outbuilding on the farmland known as The Red Barn.

The description of eyewitnesses of that shadowy figure in frock coat and hat near the house matches William Corder exactly. And the *easterly* direction the ghost took leads directly to the cottage where the ill-fated Maria lived, not far from the barn where the couple were to meet. To local people then - and today - the evidence is overwhelming: the ghost of William Corder had returned to play out the dramatic events that have made the killing in this quiet, rural corner of Suffolk famous all over the world.

The story of the murder in the Red Barn and the haunting at the farmhouse are, of course, familiar to everyone in Polstead and especially fascinating to the crime novelist, Ruth Rendell, who lives in a picturesque sixteenth century house set amidst eleven rolling acres in the village. Ruth's perception of the human mind and of the horror that lies beneath the trivia of apparently everyday lives has made her books international best sellers.

"There is supposed to be a sinister atmosphere in this area," Miss Rendell says, citing the number of real-life crimes that have taken place in the district in recent years, including the murder of doctor's wife Diana Jones; the shooting by antique dealer Wilfred Bull of his wife; and the mass-slaughter by Jeremy Bamber of the members of his family. "There are also a lot of haunted houses and ghosts here. Polstead Rectory was said to be the most haunted rectory on the Church's books, and the Red Barn murderer, Corder, is said to haunt the farmhouse where he lived. I don't feel it myself, but I think there may be something in it." (As a matter of interest, Ruth has utilised her local knowledge of the supernatural, thinly disguised, in what I think is one of her best short stories, "The Haunting of Shawley Rectory" which she published in 1979.)

Others in the village I have spoken to are rather more positive about the haunting, but quite often divided in their opinions as to Corder's guilt in the Red Barn Murder. Some accept the general verdict of history that he disposed of the mistress who had become a liability to him and his social ambitions; others feel he was trapped by a promiscuous and unscrupulous young lady who wanted to better herself, and that he only killed her accidentally during a quarrel in the barn. It was these differing opinions - plus the lack of an available popular history of the crime - which prompted this book, now reappearing in a new edition twelve years after its initial publication.

Fascination with the Red Barn Murder is as keen now - not to mention as world-wide - as it has been for decades, probably matched only in popularity in the annals of Victorian crime by the 'Master Cracksman' Charley Peace and the infamous Jack the Ripper. Writing recently, crime historian Colin Wilson said, "The Maria Marten murder has long been the subject of ballads and stage melodramas, and romanticised versions of it still appear in the more lurid of women's journals."

I can go even further than that from my own experience. A few years ago in Chicago, the 'gangster city' of America, I was asked all about the story while staying with some relatives whose only knowledge of the part of Suffolk in which I lived was the murder of young Maria by the "wicked squire" William Corder. And while in Australia recently visiting the old Melbourne Goal which is kept as a shrine to the famous 'ironclad' bushranger, Ned Kelly, I was asked if it was *really* true that Maria's body had been found as a result of a dream experienced by her mother.

In Germany, I am informed, crime enthusiasts are attracted to the legend because Maria was dressed in men's clothing for her fatal tryst with her lover, while the French are intrigued by all the letters which Corder received when, after doing away with his mistress, he unashamedly advertised in the London newspapers for a wife! For the Japanese, the greatest interest apparently lies in the book of the trial which is bound in a piece of skin taken from Corder's corpse and which is now on show in Bury St. Edmunds.

Hardly a year seems to pass without a new version of the old stage play, *The Red Barn Murder*, being performed somewhere in the world; a mention of the case being made on radio or television; and sometimes even an adaptation of the legend in a book or novel. Indeed, on the 150th anniversary of the Corder trial, *The Times* reprinted a full-column extract from its original report which it had considered of such interest as to devote more than half of its four broadsheet pages! So timeless, in fact, has the story become that some publishers have had no qualms in updating the story - like the Mellifont paperback illustrated in these pages with Corder and

Maria dressed in fashions of the nineteen-thirties.

Rather more credit is due to author Terry Deary for his historical paperback novel, *The Real Maria Marten* (1979), in which an intrepid London reporter, George Moon, of the *London Weekly*, is sent to Suffolk in 1828 to cover the case and there discovers that the evidence against Corder is contradictory at best and cruelly biased at worst. The plot is also enlivened by Moon's determination to try and save Corder from the gallows by dressing up as the Rector of Polstead and attempting to smuggle him out of Bury Jail. I give even higher marks to Peter Lovesey, the creator of those two popular Victorian television detectives, Cribb and Sergeant Cork, whose excellent short story, *The Corder Figure* (1985), utilised one of the now highly collectable earthenware figures of Corder and Maria which were manufactured as souvenirs at the time in a story about frustrated love and murder in which the statue ultimately brings the killer to justice.

The legend has also become something of a favourite topic among lecturers of famous crimes, not the least of these being former Detective Inspector Wrates of Scotland Yard, who has made a special study of the case based on papers and documents he has had access to at the Yard. And a campaign to actually clear Corder's name of the murder is being carried out by a Bury St. Edmunds' historian, Leslie Sheen, who has assembled evidence to support his claim that the crime was, in fact, an accident, and he has petitioned both his local MP and the Home Secretary - so far unavailingly - to have the court verdict overturned.

These and other examples all serve to emphasise the public's fascination with the Polstead murder - a fascination which every year brings increasing numbers of visitors from all over the world to look at the remaining buildings where the drama was enacted. Unfortunately, while Corder's House, Maria Marten's cottage and Polstead Church (where she was buried) have survived, the Red Barn is no more, although similar barns are a not unfamiliar sight in the district. There are even some rather gruesome artifacts, including a bust of Corder, the pistols he is said to have used to kill Maria, and the book bound in his skin, all on display at Moyse's Hall Museum in Bury St. Edmunds.

Not far from this museum, on the outskirts of Bury alongside the main road to Sudbury, stands the front facade of the jail where Corder stepped into eternity when he was publicly hung in full view of thousands

THE RED BARN,

A TALE,

FOUNDED ON FACT.

LONDON
PRINTED FOR KNIGHT AND LACEY,
1828.

(Above) William Maginn's book published shortly after Corder's execution which helped to create the enduring legend of the murder in the Red Barn.

(Left) The Red Barn Murder has been transposed to the twentieth century in this extraordinary Mellifont paperback book.

AN

AUTHENTIC AND FAITHFUL HISTORY

OF THE

MYSTERIOUS MURDER

OF

MARIA MARTEN,

WITH

A FULL DEVELOPMENT OF ALL THE EXTRAORDINARY CIRCUMSTANCES WHICH
LED TO THE DISCOVERY OF HER BODY IN

The Red Barn;

TO WHICH IS ADDED, THE

TRIAL OF WILLIAM CORDER,

TAKEN AT LARGE IN SHORT HAND SPECIALLY FOR THIS WORK,

WITH

AN ACCOUNT OF HIS EXECUTION, DISSECTION, &c.

AND

MANY INTERESTING PARTICULARS RELATIVE TO THE VILLAGE OF
POLSTEAD AND ITS VICINITY;

THE PRISON CORRESPONDENCE OF CORDER,

AND

FIFTY-THREE LETTERS, IN ANSWER TO HIS ADVERTISEMENT FOR A WIFE.

THE WHOLE COMPILED AND ARRANGED WITH UPWARDS OF THREE HUNDRED
EXPLANATORY NOTES,

By J. CURTIS,

AND EMBELLISHED WITH MANY HIGHLY INTERESTING ENGRAVINGS.

"A pick-axe and a spade, a spade ;   A pit of clay for to be made
Oh! for a shrouding sheet,   For such a guest is meet."—*Shakspeare*,
    "All shudder'd at the black account,
    And scarce believ'd the vast amount."—*Cotton*.

LONDON:
PUBLISHED BY THOMAS KELLY, PATERNOSTER-ROW.

MDCCCXXVIII.

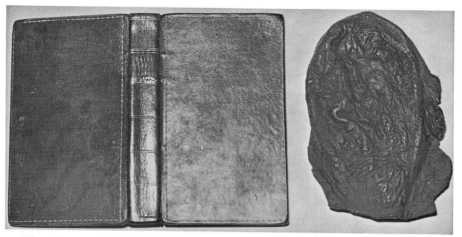

The title page (opposite) and covers (above) of James Curtis' account of the murder, bound in a piece of Corder's skin, which has become a focus of interest for Japanese students of the story.

(Below) (left) William Corder's death mask and, (right), a rare example of the earthenware figurine of the Red Barn Murder made for sale as a souvenir in the immediate aftermath of Corder's trial and execution.

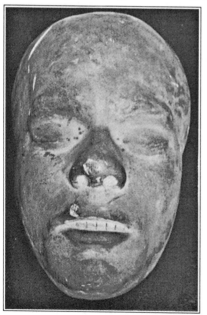

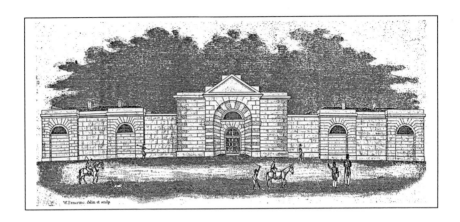

(above) Bury Jail in 1828. By 1992 (below) only the facade remains providing the rear wall of a small development of town houses.

of spectators on August 11, 1828. For many years thereafter the unhappy man's skeleton was used as a teaching aid at the old West Suffolk Hospital in the town, but since 1949 it has been in the possession of the Hunterian Museum run by the Royal College of Surgeons in London, to whom it was given to ensure its preservation. There the bones of the man who began a legend in one moment of madness hang to this day. Unacknowledged, and known simply as just one of "four college criminals."

But if all that remains of William Corder, Squire of Polstead and the Murderer of the Red Barn, enjoys so little recognition in its last resting place, quite the opposite is true of the events which he initiated over 165 years ago . . .

Polstead in 1828, the year of the Red Barn murder.

1

The Crime of the Century

* * *

T HE STORY of the murder in the Red Barn has been called one of the most famous melodramas in the world.

On first examination it seems little more than the rather sordid murder of a country girl by a singularly brutal local landowner who, having fathered an illegitimate child by her, then destroyed her before she could ruin his reputation. The only unusual element was that the crime was discovered and the criminal punished as a result of the victim's stepmother having a dream which revealed the secret hiding place of the corpse in a barn.

But such are only the barest details of a remarkable tale that has become a legend over the past one hundred and sixty-five years, familiar to millions of people all over the world.

The killing of the village beauty Maria Marten by the young squire, William Corder, in the charming, almost isolated village of Polstead in Suffolk in May 1827, has a good claim to be the best-known murder committed in the nineteenth century. It has also every right to be seen as the archetypal human drama of the innocent maiden betrayed by the well-to-do villain - and further, the distinction of being the most extraordinary instance ever of a murder solved by a prophetic dream.

Because we are looking back at these events across such a wide gulf of time, it is easy for the cynic to claim that the story is now mostly myth, a virtual Gothic fantasy woven out of half-truths, village gossip and the public's insatiable thirst for scandal. But such a view is speedily overthrown when one turns up the comment of the Magistrate, Matthew Wyatt, who committed Corder for trial after his arrest in London:

"I never knew or heard of a case in my life which abounded with so many extraordinary incidents as the present. It really appears more like a romance than a tale of common life, and were it not that the circumstances were so well authenticated, it would appear absolutely incredible. It, however, verifies the remark of Lord Byron that 'Truth is stranger than fiction'."

How this initial realisation of the unique character of the murder was later substantiated and developed has been succinctly described by Maurice Willson Disher in his book, *Blood & Thunder: Mid-Victorian Melodrama and its Origins* (1949):

"In the chronicles of capital punishment the words 'for the murder of his paramour' or 'for the murder of his concubine' are often recorded. Scores of such deeds have been forgotten. One, the killing of Maria Marten, mole-catcher's daughter, by William Corder in the Red Barn, Polstead, has become a legend. Puppets, peep-shows and ballad-mongers recognised it at once as matter for entertainment. Writers of condemned-men's confessions and full reports of trials came next, with illustrated histories published in sixpenny parts. Novelists elaborated the dry facts into penny dreadfuls and hacks at out-of-the-way theatres made Corder into the public's favourite villain . . ."

Today, there are in existence at least ten different versions of the melodrama and these are constantly being performed not only in Britain, but throughout the world in places as far flung as America, Australia and South Africa. The play is also a great favourite in Europe, especially in France where it is regarded as a classic example of *Grand Guignol*, and Germany where the sexual undertones are particularly stressed. Perhaps most surprisingly of all, it is occasionally staged in Japan where Maria Marten appears as a geisha girl and Corder as a warrior who despatches her with a huge samurai sword!

It is easy enough to understand from such facts how the view has grown that the story is mostly fiction, and indeed the modern visitor to delightful Polstead, nestling almost equidistant between Colchester and Sudbury in the rolling Suffolk countryside, may well find it hard to believe that such a dastardly crime was enacted amidst such tranquility. Before we go on with the story I think, therefore, that it is worth describing the place as it is today so that the drama which unfolded there may be more clearly pictured and understood.

The village of Polstead, meaning 'a place of pools' after the two ponds separating the houses and the parish church of St. Mary's, has existed since very early times and the discovery of Roman coins has pointed to its occupation by those invaders. Sited on the northern slopes of the River Box, the village stretches across some four thousand acres, although it contains only 260 houses and a population of approximately 650 souls. Even this, though, amounts to quite a development since 1827, the year of our story, as a report in *The Sunday Times* of April 27, 1828, tells us:

"The village is an exceedingly obscure one, and does not contain more than from 20 to 30 houses. The residence of the prisoner's mother (Mrs. Corder) is, perhaps, the best building in the place. It is a neat, moderately-sized whitewashed building, with a door in the centre, and stands about midway on the hill leading from Stoke onto the Green, where the village public house called the Cock is situate. The barn where the body was deposited, and where it is the opinion the murder was committed, lies about half a mile to the left of the village. With the exception of two small cottages (one of the Marten's), distant about 100 yards, there are no buildings for a quarter of a mile around."

On entering the village any visitor is immediately struck by its neatness and charm, and indeed it recently won an award as a best-kept village. Should the visitor be arriving in Spring, then the area will undoubtedly be swathed in the white petals of the many cherry trees the village boasts. Once Polstead was famous for its annual Cherry Fair, held on the first Wednesday following July 16, and a crucial event in our story occurred on this day as we shall see later. (The cherries which grow in such abundance are known as 'Polstead Blacks' and according to an old account "are of a refined and exceptional flavour which no one has succeeded in reproducing elsewhere".)

Dominating the hill that sweeps up from the ponds which give the village its name can be seen the roof and timbered frontage of Street Farm, or 'Corder's House' as it is better known. It was in this sixteenth century farmhouse that the Corder family lived, and its appearance has changed little since the days of their occupancy. The house is full of rambling passageways, lobbies and heavily-beamed rooms, including several attics once used as servants' quarters, and the whole place has a superb view out across the rockeried gardens and adjoining countryside. In this garden is

23

A rare photograph taken in 1897 showing what little had been left by souvenir hunters of Maria Marten's grave - and a photograph of the wooden plaque which is now her only memorial.

The church of St. Mary's, Polstead has changed very little since 1828.

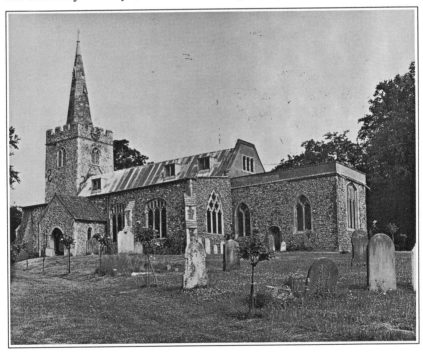

William Corder's house as it looks today.

a prolific old cherry tree and also a vast Welsh walnut tree which is believed to be over 500 years old. The various outbuildings and stables have also changed little since William Corder, his father and brothers farmed the surrounding land.

From Corder's House one can get a glimpse of St. Mary's Church nestling behind the trees on the opposite hillside beyond the pond. Among these trees stands the famous Gospel Oak believed to be 1,300 years old and a sure sign the locality was once an important meeting place. The church is twelfth century in origin with later additions, and has the only surviving old stone spire in Suffolk. It was in the graveyard surrounding the church that Maria Marten was buried in 1828, but her original gravestone has now disappeared as a result of generations of souvenir hunters who chipped away pieces of the stone until nothing remained. The old copy of a rare photograph taken in 1897 shows the correct location of her grave, but nowadays her fame is recorded on a plain tablet positioned on the small wooden building at the rear of the church, her only memorial.

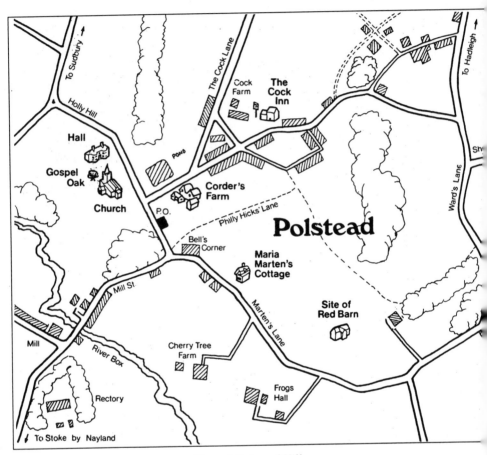

Map of Polstead Village

A sketch of Maria Marten's home made in the year of her murder.

The cottage where Maria lived with her father, stepmother and brothers and sisters is about a quarter of a mile from the church, reached by walking along Marten's Lane (which was so named after the famous murder). It is still a typical, picturesque thatched cottage which has been carefully maintained and though the modern accoutrements in its small rooms would no doubt amaze the humble family of the mole catcher who once lived there, the place has lost none of its charm as the contemporary photograph and old engraving clearly show. The vegetable garden which Maria tended with such care still exists and no doubt she spent many a happy hour as a child playing beneath the tall elm trees which stand like sentinels at the entrance to the cottage.

Continuing up this same lane the visitor comes to the last of the famous localities in our story - Barn-field Hill, close by the quaintly named Frog's Hall. Here some eighty yards back from the narrow road stood the Red Barn. I say stood, because the barn itself has long since disappeared, although because other barns of a similar description are to be found in the vicinity, many visitors mistakenly believe they have seen the original.

Nonetheless we have several representations of the original still extant and they give a pretty good idea of what it looked like.

Although it is widely assumed that the barn earned its name as a result of the bloodshed that occurred within its walls, in fact it had been known by this name for years beforehand. The reason for this is quite eerie in the context of what subsequently happened. There is an old belief in this part of Suffolk that because the daylight is so strong - and evidence of this can be found in the way it inspired such famous painters as Gainsborough, Turner and, of course, Constable - it has the ability to spotlight any localities that are inherently evil. So, at sunset, if the rays of the dying sun throw a red swatch over any building it is believed by the local people to be a warning that no good will ever happen there. And in Polstead it had been noted for years how the sun often bathed the barn on Corder's land with a glow that was as crimson-dark as blood.

A recent photograph of Maria Marten's pretty little cottage.

But to return to our story. It is hardly surprising that because of the enormous public interest that developed in the Red Barn following the disclosures of what had happened, that in the months following Corder's trial and execution, many thousands of people journeyed especially to see the building. It has been estimated that before the end of 1828, something like a quarter of a million people had come to Polstead (some even from abroad), and such was their appetite for souvenirs of this grim drama, that they all but stripped the barn of its timbers! Even when an attempt was made to stop this wholesale destruction by putting a guard on the gate leading to the barn, this was only partly effective, for the really determined souvenir hunters returned after darkness to creep around the back of the premises and, unobserved, strip off small pieces of the planks or boards. There is a story that one promoter actually offered to buy up the beams of the barn and turn them into 'Red Barn Snuff Boxes', but apparently his offer was rejected! (One type of souvenir that *was* sold with some success in the area were items of 'criminal crockery' allegedly made from local clay. According to *Notes and Queries* of November 16, 1901, these were "crude, vulgar, coarsely-coloured chinaware" depicting scenes from the murder in the Red Barn.)

In any event, it is clear that the barn was besieged by the curious and the hole from which Maria's body had been taken was left exposed for some months after the discovery. By the time these hordes had thinned somewhat, the barn was only a shadow of its former self, and had also become regarded locally as a sinister landmark. As Donald McCormick wrote in his book, *The Red Barn Mystery* (1967):

"The barn's wild and uncared-for hulk, mutilated by souvenir hunters, was a melancholic and forbidding object on a dark and tempestuous night, its timbers creaking eerily in the wind, and many villagers were frightened to go past it after nightfall in case they encountered Maria's ghost, or worse, that of Corder himself."

In the end Providence took a hand to rid the district of what had become a blot on the landscape: a fire mysteriously developed one night in 1842 and burned the place to the ground. Whether there was any human agency in the starting of this blaze it has been impossible to establish, and now even the site has disappeared beyond all trace under agricultural land.

Today the villagers of Polstead treat enquiries about the legend of the

Red Barn with kindly tolerance, several of them from the older families knowing a good many of the facts of the case from forebears who were alive at the time. They have told me with quiet amusement about the many false assumptions visitors have about the story, the most particular of them being that William Corder was a hard-hearted landlord who owned the cottage in which the Marten family lived (he did not) and that Maria sacrificed her innocence to him in a vain attempt to save her aged parents from being evicted from their cottage for non-payment of rent (which she did not). These villagers are in no doubt that she was Polstead's "good time girl" and Corder was a weak-minded, rather foolish young man who fell prey to his own character and the temptations of lust.

This, though, is just one of the variations which surround the story, and as I live in close proximity to Polstead (in the adjoining parish of Boxford) it has become increasingly evident to me that it was high time to re-examine the evidence and retell the story of the murder for a whole new generation of readers. The facts and the fiction seemed to have become so entwined and confused over the years, that no simple version of the events

A sketch of the Red Barn at Polstead from around the time of the murder.

that one turned to told the same story. After such a long space of time, of course, it is not possible to be absolutely sure that every detail is correct, but what follows is, I believe, a fairly exact and authentic account of the Murder in the Red Barn and its outcome. It is not an account embellished with theories, I hasten to add, for such arguments demand more space than a book such as this, aimed at a popular readership, can afford. These ideas as to whether or not Corder *was* guilty of the murder, or if there were any extenuating circumstances, I have, though, mentioned briefly but with sufficient information of additional sources that the interested reader can pursue them elsewhere.

What, in a nutshell, I have set out to do in the pages which follow is to try and show how what was basically an unpleasant village killing has become *the* crime of the last century. The facts, I believe you will find, present an amazing and melodramatic story of buried passions . . .

Maria Marten

Contemporary sketches of the main protagonists in the legend
(Reproduced by kind permission Radio Times Hulton Picture Library)

William Corder

2

The Village Beauty & the Wicked Squire

* * *

T HE TWO central characters in the tale of The Red Barn were actually far removed from the stereotypes that have been depicted in the legend passed down to us in melodrama, film, novel and essay over the past 165 years. Maria Marten was just *not* the virtuous village beauty callously seduced and then murdered when she had served her purpose; *nor* was William Corder, her lover, the black-hearted local squire bent on debauchery and crime. Such simplifications have come about for several reasons which we shall go into later, yet notwithstanding the real facts, Maria and Corder are now regarded around the world - wherever the tale is told, in fact - as the archetypal demure, cruelly-wronged maiden and moustacheod, unscrupulous squire of melodrama. Indeed, many differing dramatisations take them as their models; and not a few of these plays are unashamedly based on what their authors imagined had happened under the decaying roof of the Red Barn at Polstead in 1827. The facts, as I shall now set out to show, make for rather different, and perhaps even more fascinating, reading.

Whatever else we may find to be disputed about Maria Marten, of one thing there is absolutely no doubt; she was a pretty, even beautiful young girl. At the time of the terrible events which form the core of the story she was evidently quite irresistible to men, and one of her first lovers, Peter Mathews, went on record as saying she was "the greatest charmer I ever met." Leaving aside even the bias of a former lover, the most authentic engraving of her shows that she had a round face, bright, sparkling eyes, and a rather sensuous mouth. Her complexion was described as blooming, she had long brown hair worn in tresses, and of her body it was modestly said she was "of fine form and figure". Clearly even in the poor garments which she might be expected to wear, coming from a humble background, she was a striking young woman who would have caught the eye of any man, commoner or nobleman. This was a fact she was evidently aware of herself from an early age.

Maria was born on July 24, 1801, the eldest of the four children of Thomas Marten and his wife, Grace, who lived in a tiny cottage in Polstead. Mr. Marten was the local mole-catcher, an occupation that, though quite highly regarded in the community, reimbursed him poorly and he was forced to sell the produce of his garden to keep his household. The family's financial problems probably account for the fact that Maria was put into service as a maid to a clergyman at nearby Layham when she was just seven years old. This did, though, present her with the opportunity to learn to read and write (the clergyman liked to educate his household) and also for the first time to wear some pretty dresses cast off by her employer's young daughters. The impact on her personality of such modest finery was to have far-reaching effects: from that moment on Maria longed to be a lady of fashion.

It is apparent that Maria remained at Layham until her early teens when, according to conflicting reports, she was dismissed for "levity of behaviour and an inordinate love of fine clothes" or alternatively went home to look after the other three younger children in her family when her mother died. In either case, it was most evident that she did not take easily to being a housekeeper and was off at every opportunity flirting with the village lads. The picture of her so widely presented at this time as a "little mother" seems very far from the truth. Nonetheless she did stick by the younger members of the family, and this state of affairs remained unchanged for some years until, in her late teens, her father married again: to a local woman named Anne, who was just as attractive as Maria - and only a few years older. It was soon evident that the two women could not live in peace under the same roof, and Maria began making her plans to outdo her mother - she may well have been scornful of someone so young marrying a middle-aged person like her father - and at the same time to try and find a husband from a rather better station than the young men of Polstead. This is not to say she did not encourage local admirers - indeed she soon got the reputation of being rather a tease - but she was planning to save herself for someone who was not only handsome, but also of wealth and position.

Maria had better reason than most of her village contemporaries to believe she was destined for higher things for, according to a local story, she had had her future read when she was sixteen by a gypsy fortune-teller who came to Polstead. Appparently this woman informed her that although she was not destined to live to an old age, she would have many lovers and that 'riches lay within her grasp.' The gypsy told her to particularly look out for a man riding on a grey horse, for his future was bound up with hers. To the young and impressionable Maria - her mind fed on romantic notions of love - this mysterious figure was obviously going to prove the wealthy and important husband she yearned for.

When time passed and this man on horseback did not materialise, the pretty young girl could restrain her impatience no longer. Although she had already taken to playing the field and staying out late at night, she did not actually give up her virginity until she was eighteen, and then to one Thomas Corder, the son of the leading farmer of Polstead, John Corder. She could have had no idea, though, as she succumbed to the young man's groping advances in one of his father's fields, that she had formed the first family. Thomas was widely regarded as the favourite of Squire Corder's four sons and was expected to take over the farm land on his death. As she

The gypsy fortune teller who prophesied that Maria Marten would soon meet a handsome lover . . .

submitted, Maria no doubt fondly imagined herself becoming his wife and one of the leading ladies of the district. Thomas, for his part, certainly had no such intentions and the success of his seduction may well have confirmed in his mind that the stories about Maria being promiscuous were indeed true.

In any event, Maria became pregnant just before her nineteenth birthday and when she confronted Thomas with the news he straightaway insisted that his family would never allow him to marry her. However, he did promise to provide her with financial aid for the child after it was born. Though Maria was undoubtedly disappointed at such an announcement, she did not betray her lover, and no doubt fortuitously for both of them the child died a few weeks after its birth, and was quietly buried in Polstead Church. Young Thomas Corder thereafter scrupulously avoided any further contact with his former mistress.

Maria, too, quickly got over the disapproval of her father and also turned a deaf ear to what was being gossipped about her in the village. Indeed all such thoughts fled from her mind when, a short while after her baby's death, true to the gypsy's prophecy, the man on a grey horse came riding into her life at the annual Polstead Cherry Fair. He proved to be Peter Mathews, a visitor from London and related to the owner of Polstead Hall. A tall, handsome man, middle-aged and with a natural weakness for women, he saw and accepted the unspoken invitation in Maria Marten's eyes as he rode by. Within a matter of hours she was in bed with him in a hotel in Ipswich and indulging in what was to prove the first of a whole series of such illicit meetings.

From the start Mathews left Maria in no doubt that he was not the marrying kind, but he did spend money on her and bought her fine clothes as well as introducing her for the first time to London society. Naive as she was of the ways of the big city, her beauty proved the passport to places and excitements she had only dreamed of before. And when she fell pregnant once again, Mathews was quick to settle an allowance of five pounds a quarter on her and the child when it was born. Perhaps this regular source of income was the reason why Maria was allowed to return home to have the child - a boy named Thomas Henry - for such a sum undoubtedly helped supplement the Marten family's meagre resources.

Even the fact that she had now borne two illegitimate children, and it must have become increasingly clear to her that a promiscuous life was not the way to lure gentlemen to the altar, Maria had obviously gained a taste for the high life which she was not willingly prepared to give up. She spent more time away from Polstead - living it up in Ipswich, Bury St. Edmunds and occasionally London - and to many villagers she seemed a prostitute in all but the fact that she took no money directly from her lovers. They merely provided a roof over her head and food for her stomach in return for her favours. However, whenever she felt in need of a break she returned briefly to her father's cottage and her growing infant son.

No doubt this life style might have continued for a good many years more, until the loss of her looks no longer made her sexually attractive to men and thereby deprived her of her sole means of support. It is no more than a matter of conjecture, though - for in fact, in the early months of 1826, still a beauty, she met another of the Corder sons, William, and began an association which gave rise to the events still famous to this day . . .

* * *

William Corder was the third of John Corder's four sons - John jnr., Thomas, William and James; and there were also two daughters, Mary and Jane. John Corder senior was a hard-working farmer who ran his life by strict Christian principles. A regular churchgoer, he ruled his children with a firm hand and administered his three hundred-acre holding with exemplary diligence. If he had a fault in an age when fathers believed their offspring should be governed with discipline rather than love, it was that he favoured Thomas at the expense of his other children, both younger and older. For a reason which has never been explained, he seems to have liked William least of all.

William's appearance certainly did not favour him greatly as more than one contemporary print has shown, but it is probably equally true that none of the Corders were oil paintings. Undoubtedly, though, he did not deserve the epithet which was put on him *after* his trial that 'there was always something sinister about the man as though he had the mark of a monster on him'. He was a short man, just under five feet five inches tall, lightly built, and with the added complication for a small person of having a stoop. His round face was spotted with freckles and his nose with its pronounced turned-up end tended to give him an expression of slight stupidity whenever he smiled. But this belied an alert and intelligent mind, although one which could be devious and cunning by turn.

William was born at some time in 1803 (the precise date is unknown), and because of the active dislike in which he was held by his father, grew up close to his mother. This situation no doubt played a part in shaping his character as he sought for ways to avoid the anger of his father; and his life was not made easier by the fact that because of his background he was far from popular at the village school and was nick-named "Foxey". Later, he was transferred to a private school at Hadleigh where he stayed for three years, surprising everybody by distinguishing himself with his all-round educational ability and particular skill at composition. Perhaps predictably, he nursed an ambition to become either a writer or a teacher.

But John Corder had no intention that his out-of-favour son should enter any such profession: at sixteen years old he was abruptly brought back to Polstead and set to work on the farm. This fact, plus being paid no more than a common labourer, nurtured the seeds of discontent in the young man's mind. It seems likely that soon after this he began committing little thefts and frauds to obtain enough money to enjoy himself during his few spare hours. This enjoyment took the form of illicit drinking with a small group of cronies in the local inn, 'The Cock', and dalliances with certain of the local girls of easy virtue. He is believed to have had his first sexual encounter at sixteen with a girl whom he took in one of his father's pea

The unprepossessing figure of William Corder who was to make the gypsy's prediction come true in a most unexpected manner.

fields. After the encounter, he is said to have generously sent the girl home with an armful of the vegetables!

In such a small community as Polstead, and with a father of such unbending principles as John Corder, it is not surprising that when word of William's indiscretions reached his parent, he was immediately and sternly taken to task. For punishment he was sent up to London where he was told to enlist in the Merchant Navy which, the older Corder believed, would correct his failing character. Unfortunately, though, Corder was refused enlistment because of his bad eyesight.

Now 22 years old, William was in no mood to return immediately to Polstead - especially as he had a little money in his pocket which his father had given him - and he was anxious to sample life in London. Naturally enough, he quickly gravitated to the brothels, drinking places and gambling dens which drew all such young men from the country like magnets.

During his sojourn in the Capital, William Corder formed particular friendships with three people, all of whom were to play significant roles in his ill-fated future. The first was a beautiful, dark-haired schemer and whore named Hannah Fandango (there are reasonable doubts as to whether this was, in fact, her real name), an unsavoury criminal known as Samuel 'Beauty' Smith and one Thomas Griffiths Wainewright, a forger, writer and ultimately a poisoner who was later immortalised as Slinkton in Charles Dickens' story *Hunted Down* (1860). All three influenced his character to varying degrees.

It was Hannah Fandango whom Corder met first, in all probability while she was plying her trade as a prostitute. The daughter of a sea captain and a mother of Creole descent, Hannah had run away from a London boarding school while still only fourteen and plunged into the Capital's low-life, first as an actress then as mistress to a series of men-about-town. But her constant infidelities made even these tolerant playboys abandon her, and in time she was forced to turn to prostitution and crime. Her criminal activities consisted mainly of being part of a network smuggling in contraband goods from the Continent and, to this end, she maintained a small dwelling about a mile from Polstead. When William Corder encountered her and discovered this common link, the lonely young man up from the country was already half under her spell. Her bewitching beauty and skill at love-making completed the task of bringing him totally

(Left) The Cock Inn in Polstead today. It was here that Corder and his cronies would drink and make merry.

into her power. He, for his part, was convinced he had found the love of his life.

An interesting suggestion has been made, by the bye, that Hannah Fandango disguised her smuggling activities in Suffolk by posing as a gypsy fortune-teller - and that it was *she* who made the prophecy to Maria Marten that she would meet a man on a grey horse! If this were true, then by so doing she set in motion the chain of events which culminated in the murder in the Red Barn. Unfortunately, though, there are no facts to substantiate the story.

Anybody who associated with Hannah Fandango for periods of time longer than it took to commit the sex act needed money to indulge her whims and expensive tastes, and William Corder quickly ran through his small allowance trying to keep his new love satisfied. Once this was gone, she no doubt urged him to get more, and after what seems likely to have been several half-hearted attempts trying to exploit his penchant for writing by endeavouring to get work on newspapers, he was ripe to be encouraged into criminal ways. To this end, Hannah introduced him to 'Beauty' Smith, a member of the Suffolk ring to which she belonged, and also a man who lived in the Polstead district from time to time. As a matter of fact, Corder may already have known of Smith by reputation for he had several times been in trouble for the theft of livestock in the area and actually been imprisoned for this on a number of occasions.

Smith knew London like the back of his hand and was an expert at all the dubious pastimes of the Capital such as gambling and card-sharping. He was always willing to guide any young buck anxious to sample the flesh-pots of the Capital, helping the man to spend his resources and taking his own cut either from the 'managements' to whom he introduced his clients or else when the unfortunate victim was insensible from drink. He procured for several prostitutes too, and was in all probability Hannah Fandango's protector. Under his influence, combined with that of Hannah, Corder was soon immersed in London low-life and easily led into their devious schemes. Although it is difficult to pin any particular crime to his name at this time, he almost certainly took part in duping card players and obtained sums of money from his father by fraud with stories that he was setting himself up in business. All such cash was spent wildly on the faithless Hannah.

It was at this time that Corder met the third member of the trio of people who became his principal London friends, Thomas Wainewright (1794-1847), the critic and painter who, when his spending outstripped his means, turned to poisoning members of his family to restore his finances. He flitted between the worlds of letters and crime, alternately publishing

The painter-turned-poisoner Thomas Griffiths Wainewright who was to have a considerable influence on Corder's life, and was later immortalised as Slinkton in Charles Dickens' story of crime and murder, 'Hunted Down'.

Corder being introduced into London low-life by Thomas Wainewright and 'Beauty' Smith - an illustration from The Red Barn by William Maginn (1828).

criticisms and articles under the pen-name Janus Weathercock, and at other times perpetrating the frauds which were finally to lead to him being sentenced to transportation to Australia - his activities as a poisoner remained undiscovered. It was Hannah who first introduced Corder to Wainewright at a time when he still had slight hopes of becoming a writer. Although Wainewright could do little for the young man from Suffolk, the two did become friends of a kind, and later in his life when exiled in Australia, Wainewright was quite willing to talk about his friendship. In a letter written to an English correspondent, Caroline Palmer, and quoted by Donald McCormick in *The Red Barn Mystery*, he says of this association:

> "He came to me from the Suffolk countryside, a stooping youth with Napoleonic gestures and a sense of drama. I think he wanted to dramatise himself. He wanted to write, but he was, shall we say, more a Satyr than a satirist, fonder of words than they were of him... He was introduced to me by a young woman named Hannah Fandango, a dancer whom I often painted. She was an astonishing creature, delightful but wicked, seductive but unscrupulous, who lived like some medieval adventuress, a Lucretia Borgia

of the stews. It was always so odd to learn that so essentially a town person should spend some of her life living in a hut in Suffolk."

"On the subject of forgery," he went on, "I may not be entirely guiltless of having implanted some ideas in Corder's mind. He often complained about being kept short of funds by his father and I recall telling him that such treatment was foolish because it encouraged forgery and I explained how very easy it was to forge cheques and remain undetected - at least for a considerable period."

Of what ultimately happened to Corder, he added: "He was obviously, in retrospect, a far more complex and interesting character than I gave him credit for . . . I find it hard to believe he was a cold and calculating murderer. It would have surprised me much less to have learned that some woman had actually killed him."

Wainewright also claimed to have been present at a terrible quarrel which finally ended the relationship between Hannah and Corder, but the fact of the matter seems that the constantly penniless William finally became disillusioned with his precarious and unstable life in London, coupled with the shattering of his infatuation for his mistress by discovering yet another of her infidelities, and decided on returning to Polstead, willing to eat humble pie if his father so demanded. And the old man did with a vengeance.

Conditional on William being allowed back in the family home was that he would go back to work on the land, he would refrain from drinking and mixing with undesirable company, and he would become a regular churchgoer again. Thus, in the spring of April 1824, William Corder became a simple countryman once more, thoughts of London and Hannah had to be thrust from his mind (although she was to appear again and continue as an influence on him for the rest of his days) and he was in no doubt this was his last chance to make good unless he wanted to be finally and irrevocably cut off from any kind of support from his unbending father.

All the evidence points to the fact that for the next two years Corder was, true to his agreement, a dutiful and hard-working son. He worked long hours on the land, took his turn in the business affairs of the farm, and followed religious pursuits in his limited spare time. Though his family believed him to be a reformed character, there were others who merely felt he was biding his time till the opportunity for him to return to his old ways occurred once again.

In December 1825 the first of several tragedies struck the Corder family. The old man, John Corder, died quite suddenly. Hardly had Mrs. Corder recovered from this than two of her sons, the oldest, John, and the youngest, James, both fell ill from the effects of tuberculosis and were virtual invalids thereafter. The next son in line, Thomas, manfully shouldered the responsibility for running the farm, and for a while his younger brother, William, made an able lieutenant. But with the oppressive influence of his father no longer overshadowing him, the one - time man-about-town was indeed starting to dream of former days again.

Then in the spring of 1826 he had the fateful meeting which was to so dramatically influence the course of his life for its remaining few, tragic months. He became friendly with the mischievous, seductive village beauty known as Maria Marten . . .

3

The Path to the Red Barn

* * *

A LTHOUGH William Corder had heard of Maria Marten - indeed it would be surprising if he had not in such a small place as Polstead - they had not actually met and conversed before that fateful Spring morning in 1826. Of course he knew that his older brother Thomas had had an affair with the girl which had resulted in an illegitimate child. But that was a forbidden topic in the Corder household, and certainly not something that either Thomas or their father would have discussed with him.

It was a bright morning as William strolled past the Marten's cottage on the way to some of the Corder's outlying fields. In the garden Maria was busy among the flowers and vegetables enjoying one of the few activities she liked other than the good life. Those who still had a kind word to say for her, admitted she was good at gardening and had what is known in country parlance as "green fingers". She had not long returned from a quite lengthy stay in London through most of the winter months, and although she had enjoyed the few days she had spent again getting to know her growing young son, Thomas Henry, already there were the first stirrings of restlessness in her heart as she attacked a patch of weeds beside the vegetable plot. Then out of the corner of her eye she caught sight of the unmistakable stooped figure of William Corder walking by the hedge. She knew the farmer's son by sight, and quite a bit more about him as well - mostly from village gossip. He was supposed to have been leading a wild life up in London and living with a prostitute, the wagging tongues said, but when all his money had run out he had been forced to return home like a whipped cur. As someone who had also wanted more out of life than the isolation and lack of excitement in Polstead, she couldn't help feeling a certain sympathy well up inside her for the man. When she looked up at him and their eyes met she felt something else stir inside her, too.

Although William Corder's mind had been on other things, the beguiling smile that Maria Marten gave him across her garden could not fail to capture his attention. For a moment he hesitated as if unsure whether or not to walk on. When the girl's smile was complemented with a small nod of the head and a little curtsey he knew he would have to stop and speak to her.

No-one else witnessed the first conversation between Maria and Corder, nor were there other eyes watching when they took their first evening walk together, skirting the village and the various places used by other young couples. Such indeed was the secrecy surrounding the start of their association, that neither family was to become aware they were seeing each other for several months, and by that time they had undoubtedly started being intimate, most likely in the same fields belonging to the Corder family where Maria had first given herself to Thomas Corder.

Maria, for her part, seemed to have no scruples about another association with a member of the same family, even after the unhappy result of the previous affair, and William was evidently so attracted by the beauty

It was while Maria Marten was working in the garden of her parents' cottage that she first saw William Corder . . .

and sexual dexterity of his willing new conquest - who seemed such a contrast to the unscrupulous and scheming Hannah - that what had happened in the past became of no consequence. He chose even to ignore her reputation for promiscuity. Nonetheless, he was cautious enough in his early dealings with Maria to avoid being seen with her and gave her no false promises of marriage to win her compliance. Not that it seems evident she required any: the fact that he was a man of higher station and one who would come into money eventually as well as being a fun-lover seemed to satisfy her completely for the time being.

Although for their lovemaking Corder did not treat Maria to the hotel beds of Ipswich, Bury St. Edmunds or London, as some of her previous lovers had done, he showed her greater kindness than most, and soon found a better place for their meetings than the fields - the Red Barn.

This decaying, but still usable, thatched building on the Corder estate served primarily for storing hay for the livestock, and in early spring still contained small piles of straw left over from the winter into which the young lovers could tumble. Fortuitously the barn was a place avoided by most village people at night because, as mentioned earlier, there was a time at sunset when the sinking sun bathed it in almost blood-red rays of light. This strangeness did not leave the structure after dark either, for by night its dark bulk invariably looked mysterious and sinister against the skyline. But William Corder held no such superstitious fears about the place, and evidently quickly dispelled any misgivings Maria might have had. And it was there, wrapped in straw, the silence only disturbed by the occasional rustling of nocturnal animals and the distant cry of an owl, that Maria and Corder experienced again some of the joys they had both earlier discovered in London - though both had paid dearly for the experience. The farm, his work and religion were far from Corder's thoughts at such moments as Maria filled his eyes with her naked beauty, and through the months of that summer and autumn both faded still further from his mind. He kept to his daily tasks certainly, but no more was he seen in church. Maria, too, lost her immediate desire to roam from the village.

Then, as autumn drew in around Polstead, Maria announced some news to her young lover as they lay satiated in the barn one night. Her words sent a chill through him, colder than any winter wind. She was pregnant.

After his initial shock, Corder no doubt sat silently wondering what

Corder and Maria set out for a night of love-making in the Red Barn.

on earth he could do about this state of affairs. He knew that Maria's parents would want to press him to marry their daughter, while his mother would rigorously oppose any such union. He could, of course, just deny he was responsible, for such was Maria's reputation that it would be only her word against his that he was the father and, as she had known other men, the benefit of the doubt would almost certainly be given to him. But whatever else has been said about Corder it seems clear, in hindsight, that at this time he *was* fond of Maria - may indeed have loved her - and immediately put out of his mind any thoughts of abandoning her. What he did resolve to do was to try and keep the news of the baby away from his family. Interestingly, too, from the time of this announcement, Corder began to be seen openly with Maria, although he soon afterwards began making plans for her to leave the district as soon as her swelling figure began to reveal her condition.

A couple of months later, just after Christmas, Corder found that his troubles were only just beginning. Perhaps in an effort to raise the necessary money for Maria's confinement, William intercepted one of Peter Mathews' regular five pound payments to his former mistress (for the use of her and his son, Thomas Henry) and then denied all knowledge of the money when challenged about it. When Mathews instructed a solicitor to find out what had happened to the money and the trail led inexorably to Corder, he was forced to confess to Maria that he had taken the money and to get her to exonerate him. At this time, theft and forgery were capital offences which could result at best in imprisonment, and at worst in transportation to Australia or possibly execution. It has been suggested this incident showed that Corder was already growing tired of Maria, but the details are still so obscure - what little we do know was only presented by the prosecution at Corder's trial as another example of his black-guardly character - that it is impossible to do more than conject. A further argument says that Corder may have actually murdered Maria because she knew the truth of this episode of the stolen money and was therefore in a position to expose her lover at any moment she chose if he did not do as she wanted.

The dust from this curious matter had hardly settled when William was dealt another blow. On the morning of February 23, Thomas Corder, his older brother, then just twenty five years old, was drowned in the pond immediately below the family home. The pond was frozen over at the time and Thomas had attempted to take a short cut across to catch up with a friend. He was barely half-way over when the ice cracked and he was plunged to his death in the icy water below.

As a result of Thomas's death and the ill-health of both John and James Corder, the full burden of running the family's affairs now became William's responsibility. And he had Maria to think of, too. Because of the openness of his association with her over the past few months, their alliance was known to all the villagers. But what these people did not know was that he had confessed to Maria's father and stepmother that he was the father of her unborn child. It was his intention, he told old Marten, to marry Maria when an opportune moment arose - but this was not just yet for he knew the news would upset his mother and she had had rather a lot to cope with just recently.

In order to conceal the birth from the rest of the Corders, and with Maria's agreement, William placed her in lodgings in the town of Sudbury about twelve miles away on March 19. Over the next few weeks he visited her regularly at the little house in Plough Lane where she stayed: and it was there that she gave birth to a boy child in the second week of April. A short while later, on April 16, she returned to the Marten cottage in Polstead and there kept very much to herself, her presence and that of the baby unknown to the rest of the world.

Both mother and child were in poor health, and Maria's stepmother, Anne, apparently cared for the baby during this period. However, the infant

A chilling moment for Corder and Maria as they take the body of their recently dead illegitimate child to bury in the fields. Another illustration from William Maginn's dramatic novelisation.

grew steadily weaker and died two weeks after the return from Sudbury. The cause of the death of this child has never been established, but its general poor state of health from birth and the fact it was never seen by a doctor were no doubt contributory factors.

When William Corder slipped in to see Maria the following day he was greeted with the news of his infant son's death, and at the same time further impassioned demands by the Martens for him to marry their daughter. The young man's only commitment was that he and Maria would take the little corpse to Sudbury for burial and it would be best for all concerned if nothing was said about the birth to anyone. He refused to be drawn on the other question. On the surface it would seem that one of Corder's main problems had been solved by the infant mortality, and certainly the total lack of any indication of emotion on his part underlines this point.

Two nights later the couple crept away unnoticed from the cottage, the tiny corpse in a box under William's arm. It must have been a grim and unpleasant mission on which they were bound, and all the evidence points to the fact that they did not reach Sudbury, and in all probability buried the body in the fields somewhere near Polstead. Certainly there is no record of any such burial in Sudbury. (In a number of the accounts of this episode in the story of Maria Marten the suggestion has been made that the death

50

of the child might have been due to it being conveniently poisoned by Corder, but again this is a theory that cannot be substantiated by any facts.)

At this juncture a little light relief appeared to take Corder's mind off his difficulties - in the attractive shape of Hannah Fandango, who, with her partner in crime and debauchery 'Beauty' Smith, suddenly turned up again in Polstead. All of them were seen together enjoying themselves in 'The Cock' and then going off together afterwards. As soon as news of this carousing reached the ears of Thomas Marten and his wife they were quickly on to William again about doing his duty by their daughter and marrying her. This time they would not let him off without a firm commitment.

According to a later report, William finally agreed to these demands on the morning of Sunday, May 13, apparently only insisting that they should go to Ipswich to get wed, as he had heard that the local police constable, John Balham, was in possession of a warrant for Maria's arrest on a charge of having bastard children. He thought they had better go quickly, the next day in fact, and he would save Maria from the charge by marrying her by special licence. The Martens, although alarmed by the possibility of a charge against their daughter, agreed this was the best plan and allowed the young squire to go on his way.

A fascinating reconstruction of what happened over the next few days, culminating on Friday, May 18, is given in an article *The Red Barn* in Charles Dickens' magazine, *All The Year Round* of October 1867 and I should like to quote it verbatim as it undoubtedly has the ring of authenticity about it:

> The marriage had been fixed for the Monday, but Stoke Fair had detained Corder on that day; and on Thursday his brother James had been taken dangerously ill. Such, at least, were the excuses that Corder offered Maria Marten for not keeping his promise. The girl and her mother were upstairs in their cottage when Corder came on the Friday, and abruptly proposed to instantly start for Ipswich, as he had got the licence all ready.
>
> "Come, Maria," he said, "make haste; I am going."
>
> The girl looked round, surprised at the sudden decision and peremptory tone, and replied:
>
> "How can I go at this time of the day, without anybody seeing me?"

51

But Corder was in no mood for waiting, and he answered moodily:

"Never mind, you have been disappointed many times, and shan't be again; we will go now."

"How am I to go, William?" was the girl's next question.

"You can go up," he said, "to the Red Barn, and stop till I come to you with my horse and gig."

The girl was still full of objections. The marriage was to be a clandestine one, and yet her lover was going to drive her to Ipswich in open daylight.

"I'm not ready," she said; "and how am I to order my things?"

He was ready to answer every objection. "I will take the things," he said, "in a bag, and carry them up to the barn, and then I'll come back and walk with you."

She still disliked the suddenness of the departure.

"There are none of my workmen about," he said, "in the fields or near the barn, and I am sure the coast is quite clear."

How carefully he had foreseen every difficulty! How prompt he was to remove every lingering obstacle to their immediate marriage! The old father and stepmother were not the sort of people to oppose the will of their master, their daughter's rich lover. They made no objection. Maria then put up her things - a black silk gown, black silk stockings, a Leghorn hat, and some other small necessaries, all tucked into a wicker basket and a large black velvet reticule. There had been, probably, some previous arrangement between the lovers; for Maria now produced from some secret nook a bundle of men's clothes. These she was to put on while Corder was carrying the basket and reticule in a brown holland bag to the Red Barn. Corder then left with the bag, and Maria, crying all the time, proceeded to put on her disguise - blue trousers, a striped waistcoat, and brown coat. She wore a man's hat over her three large hair-combs, and a red and yellow silk handkerchief to muffle her chin and long earrings. She had in her hand a large green cotton umbrella with a bone handle. While Maria was still dressing, stopping every now and then to cry at the suddenness of her departure, Corder returned, carrying a gun. Now, he said, all was ready.

Before the couple left the cottage, Corder assured Mrs.Marten once again that she should not worry. "Don't make yourself at all uneasy," he said , "Maria shall be my lawful wife before I return home. If I cannot be married right away, then I'll get her a place somewhere till such time as we *can* be married."

And with that the couple went out of the house, Corder leaving by the front door and Maria the back. Again let me quote from the article in *All The Year Round*:

> The lovers left about half-past twelve, stealthily by different doors. They met in the road, the stepmother saw them meet; they both got over a gate and went across the Hare-hill field, past the hedges already in bud, in the direction of the Red Barn, which was two fields distant, and where Maria's things in the brown holland bag had been left by Corder. The disguised girl, still in tears, and the sullen lover, with the odious, sly, malign face, disappeared in the distance, where the green boughs grew greyer and fainter towards the low horizon.

It was the last time they were ever seen together. It was also the very last glimpse anyone had of Maria Marten alive.

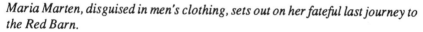

Maria Marten, disguised in men's clothing, sets out on her fateful last journey to the Red Barn.

William Corder awaits the arrival of his disguised mistress at the Red Barn. Tragedy - and an enduring place in the history of crime - is now only minutes away . . .

4

The Mystery of the Two Wives

* * *

T HERE IS an old story, still repeated occasionally in Polstead, that on the night of Friday May 18, 1827, the Red Barn was bathed in such a lurid red glow by the setting sun that it stood out like a welter of blood against the darkening horizon. The account may be nothing more than a folk tale later woven around the event that had occurred in the barn during the afternoon, but it was a fact that no-one went near the place for several weeks thereafter, nor did anyone have the faintest inkling that anything untoward had happened there that day.

No-one in Polstead, either his family or friends, saw anything of William Corder until the following Monday morning when he unexpectedly turned up again at the front door of the Marten's cottage. Anne Marten, who answered the knocking, for it was nine o'clock and her husband was already out at his work catching moles, stared in surprise at Corder for a moment. Then, recovering her voice, immediately asked where Maria was.

"I have left her at Ipswich," her caller replied. "I have got her a comfortable place. She is with a Miss Rowland who is the sister of an old school friend of mine."

Mrs. Marten remembered how her stepdaughter had left the house, then asked what Maria was doing for clothes.

"Miss Rowland has got plenty and would not let me send for any," he said, and then went on, "I have got a licence, but it must go to London to be signed, so I cannot marry until a month or six weeks. But I have changed a cheque for twenty pounds and given her the money."

Although Mrs. Marten was clearly unhappy with Corder's explanation, she had no alternative but to let him go on his way, although not before she had voiced her misgivings about the situation.

In the following weeks whenever the paths of the two people crossed, Corder continued to insist that Maria was still happy and contented with Miss Rowland in Ipswich, and was just too busy preparing for her marriage to write to her father and stepmother. Thomas Marten, for his part, was apparently inclined to accept Corder's story and for a time told his young wife to stop pestering the squire with her questions.

Although Anne Marten continued to nurse her suspicions through that summer of 1827 she had little opportunity to talk to William Corder, for further tragedy overtook the Corder family and kept him almost constantly at home or at work, and from time to time away from Polstead on related matters. The tragedy was the death within a short while of each other of his two ailing brothers, John and James, from the combined effects of tuberculosis and typhus. These two latest fatalities which had now carried off all but one of her five men folk in less than three years left Mrs. Corder a broken, almost demented old woman.

The villagers of Polstead felt some sympathy for William Corder at this time, and certainly did not share Anne Marten's concern about the continuing absence of her stepdaughter. Why, hadn't the girl disappeared before and gone galavanting up to London, the gossips muttered whenever they met. And didn't she always turn up again sooner or later like a bad penny when her latest fancy man had thrown her out? Some of them had heard tell she had last been seen with William Corder and reckoned he might have set her up as his mistress somewhere so that he could go to her whenever he chose without upsetting his mother. In any event, they weren't really *that* concerned about the young baggage.

By the autumn of 1827, Mrs. Marten had taken to dogging Corder's footsteps and questioning him about Maria whenever she could confront him. He continued to insist she was well, passed on certain messages he said she had asked him to give her family - and also her apologies for not having written due to her right hand being painful with a stiffness which prevented her putting pen to paper.

Then, almost as if to assuage the stepmother's anxiety, Corder for a time resumed his old habit of visiting the Martens' cottage whenever he returned from a trip away from Polstead. But although he seemed able to keep the parents happy, each visit seemed to him to result in progressively more vigorous cross-questioning by Mrs. Marten.

After one such confrontation, William rubbed the back of his hand wearily over his forehead and told his listeners that he was very concerned that all the extra work of the farm and travelling to and fro to see Maria was beginning to adversely affect his health. He was very much afraid if he did not take care of himself he might end up like his poor brothers.

On September 8, Corder seemingly decided to take heed of his own diagnosis (or leave Polstead before the questioning about Maria revealed too much, according to another school of thought) and went to tell the Martens he was going away from Polstead for a while. He planned to go to a health spa for recuperation, he said, and then he would rejoin Maria and finally make her his wife. In due course, he added, they would return to the Corder family home as man and wife.

It is unlikely that Mrs. Marten was any more convinced by this story of William's than any of his previous ones, although her husband again took his words at face value. And the old man believed his faith in Corder was vindicated when the following letter arrived for him dated October 18. It was from Corder and had been written from the Bull Inn in Leadenhall Street, London, informing him that he and his daughter were at last married.

"Thomas Marten," he wrote, "I am just arrived at London upon business respecting our family affairs, and am writing to you before I take the least refreshment, because I shall be in time for this night's post, as my stay in town will be short, anxious to return again to her who is now my wife, and with whom I shall be the happiest of men. I should have had her with me, but it was her wish to stay at our lodging at Newport, in the Isle of Wight, which she described to you in her letter: and we feel astonished that you have not yet answered it, thinking illness must have been the cause. In that she gave you a full description of our marriage, and that Mr. Rowland was daddy, and Miss R. bride's-maid. Likewise she told you they came with us as far as London, where we continued together very comfortable for three days, when we parted with the greatest regret. Maria and myself went on to the Isle of Wight, and they both returned home. I told Maria I should write to you directly I reached London, who is very anxious to hear from you, fearing some strange reason is the cause of your not writing."

Corder concluded the letter by saying that he planned to take a farm for them to live in on the Isle of Wight, and closed, "I think you had better burn all letters, after taking directions, that nobody may form the least idea of our residence."

When, naturally, Thomas Marten replied, he said that he was delighted with the news of their nuptuals, but neither he nor his wife had received any correspondence whatsoever from Maria. At this Corder expressed amazement and promised forthwith to initiate enquiries.

"It is, I think, very odd," he wrote by return of post, "that letters should be lost in this strange way. Was it not for the discovery of our residence, I would certainly indict the Post Office; but I cannot do that without making our appearance at a court which would be very unpleasant to us both."

Poor old Thomas Marten, the mole catcher of Polstead, may well have felt the business was odd, but in truth the only thing that would at that moment have been unpleasant for either of them was the realisation by anybody that both of Corder's letters were a pack of lies from start to finish.

* * *

Despite what he had indicated in his letters, Corder had no intention whatsoever of going to the Isle of Wight. In a nutshell he had seemingly decided to cut himself off completely from his old life in Polstead, and the letters were an attempt to finally satisfy the Martens that all was well between him and Maria and that it would be in everyone's best interests if there was no further communication between them. Believing he had achieved this, he took himself off to a quiet South Coast resort where he intended to rest and plan his future.

During his absence from London, it seems evident that Corder must have realised that one pressing need for his future was going to be money as his funds were fast dwindling and he obviously could not contact his mother in Polstead without giving away his whereabouts. His earlier attempts as a writer had not met with much success, so what alternatives were open to him to restore his finances?

Though it can only be conjecture, it seems very likely that while he was recuperating he came into contact with a number of fashionable young women of means and in them he saw a possible solution to his dilemma. What would better suit his purpose than to try and find himself a wealthy bride?

That such was indeed what went through his mind seems to be borne out by the fact that when he returned to London in November 1827 he composed the following advertisement which he duly arranged to appear in *The Morning Herald* of November 12 and *The Sunday Times* of November 25:

"MATRIMONY- A private gentleman, aged twenty-four, entirely independent, whose disposition is not to be exceeded, has lately lost chief of his family by the hand of Providence, which has occasioned discord among the remainder, under circumstances the most disagreeable to relate. To any female of respectability, who would study for domestic comfort, and is willing to confide her future happiness to one in every way qualified to render the marriage state desirable, as the advertiser is in affluence. Many happy marriages have taken place through means similar to this now resorted to. It is hoped no-one will answer this through impertinent curiosity; but should this meet the eye of any agreeable lady, who feels desirous of meeting with a sociable, tender, kind, and sympathising companion, they will find this advertisement worthy of notice. Honour and secrecy may be relied on. As some little security against idle application, it is requisite that letters may be addressed, post-paid, A.Z., care of Mr. Foster, stationer, 68, Leadenhall-street, with real name and address, which will meet with most respectful attention."

The advertisement, crude as it seems, was remarkably effective: when Corder called at the accommodation address provided by Mr. Foster, the stationer was able to hand over to him a bundle of no less than 45 replies. And when William hurried back to his lodgings to read through the letters, he soon found a much more diverse selection of correspondents than he might have hoped for - ranging from shop girls to adventuresses - and among these were several which sounded decidedly promising.

As a matter of record, Mr. Foster received a further influx of 54 letters after Corder had made his first collection, but the Suffolk farmer never returned to collect these for, as we shall see, he had already found what what he was seeking. It appears Mr. Foster must have kept these letters by for some time, for immediately after Corder's name became notorious through his trial, the enterprising stationer published the 'love letters' as a book entitled *Advertisement for Wives* (1828) deleting only the real names and addresses! A selection of some of the more interesting letters are reproduced in the appendix to this book.

Commenting on these letters, Charles Dickens' magazine, *All the*

Year Round, says: "Some were from servants, others from distressed ladies of ambiguous antecedents, dilating on their various mental qualifications, their beauty, and their favourable disposition to matrimony. One letter was from a lady who kept her own carriage, and was living in a sphere very superior to his. She requested him to attend a certain church at a certain hour, having one arm in a sling, and wearing a black handkerchief. She described the carriage in which she would come and directed him to go to a certain pew in the church where he might be opposite to her, and they might have a view of each other during the service. He mistook the hour, however, and when he went to the church he found that the service was over."

An example of the handwriting of the man who advertised for a wife. This is a facsimile of a letter Corder wrote to his mother while on his way to Bury Jail.

Amongst the letters was one from a young woman named Mary Moore, who said she lived with her widowed mother and brother. She described herself as hard-working, devoted and religious, and had recently been employed as a governess with a British family in France. There was a suggestion in the letter that Mary seemed to feel herself regarded as the provider for her mother and brother, and although she was a dutiful daughter, there was a streak of determination in her character which made her want to make a life of her own.

Corder, who we have already noted was a man quickly beguiled by a pretty face, must have believed his prayers had been truly answered when he arranged a meeting with Miss Moore at her home in Gray's Inn Terrace. Not only was she pretty with dark, soulful eyes, but quietly spoken, obviously well-educated and modest into the bargain. She was also occupying herself at the time by running a small school for young children. William's immediate attraction to Mary seems to have been reciprocated, for the couple quickly agreed to meet again. After a second meeting, Corder proposed marriage, was accepted, and a wedding thereafter took place by special licence at St. Andrews Church, Holborn, early in December.

Understandably, Corder had no intention that he and his new bride should continue under the same roof as the other two Moores, and he suggested they should move out of London - which was not good for his health, he said - and perhaps establish a new boarding school of their own, at which he would also teach? Mary obviously liked the idea, and by Christmas they had found a suitable location named Grove House, in Ealing Lane, Brentford. The couple quickly settled in and soon attracted a select group of pupils: the only fly in the ointment was that Mary's mother refused to be parted from her daughter and also moved in with them.

According to one contemporary report, the Corders now enjoyed an almost idyllic period as winter changed slowly into spring, Mary busying herself with her teaching and William helping with English and Mathematics classes as best his ability would allow. Donald McCormick described this time for us in his book, *The Red Barn Mystery*:

"In the early days of the marriage William and Mary, hand in hand, went for long walks in the country, to Kew, where Mary sometimes attended the Parish Church, to Richmond Hill and the heaths and commons of the Ealing area, then very much of a country village.

William ceased all correspondence with the Martens and cut himself completely adrift from his former life. He never went to the West End, though occasionally he visited Wainewright when the latter came to Turnham Green and once or twice took Mary along with him. 'They seemed to be living an idyllic existence,' said Wainewright. 'Corder was inordinately fond of her and was for ever praising her virtues, squeezing her hand and whispering endearments to her. He loved showing her off. She played the piano, sketched a little - nothing remarkable, but her draughtsmanship was good - and spoke admirable French.' "

Though outwardly William Corder seemed to have achieved what he wanted, indeed more than he wanted - both a wife who could support him and an attractive one, too - inwardly he was racked all the time by the nagging fear that something might go wrong. That his past might at any moment catch up with him. It was a thought he could just not throw off, as Donald McCormick again tells us:

"Early in the new year Corder's apprehensions about his whereabouts being discovered increased. He began 'to behave like a frightened man', his wife said afterwards. He went out less and less, remaining indoors sometimes for days on end. His nights were disturbed and restless, he suffered from nightmares and groaned in his sleep. Once his shouts awoke the children and terrified them".

It was, indeed, a strange twist of fate that his nights should have been so troubled at this time. For back in the place he was trying so hard to obliterate from his mind somebody else was also suffering from nightmares. Nightmares that were to have a profound effect on his future - and bring him swiftly and surely into the shadow of the hangman's noose.

5

A Dream of Murder . . . and its Sequel

* * *

W INTER NIGHTS in isolated rural districts of England in the first half of the nineteenth century were invariably cold, dismal and boring. With only candles to lighten the darkness that descended in late afternoon, wood fires to combat the cold which crept insidiously into the lath and plaster cottages long before nightfall, and no books and precious little entertainment to while away the long hours until the next dawn, it was not surprising that most people took to their beds early, whether they were tired or not.

Hardworking and industrious people like Thomas Marten, the mole catcher of Polstead, would drop into an exhausted and untroubled sleep while the night was still young. But for someone like his wife, Anne, with troublesome thoughts still invading her mind when she came to bed beside him, sleep did not come easily - and when it did was often invaded by dreams, and, on occasions, nightmares.

Ever since the afternoon when her stepdaughter, Maria, and her lover, William Corder, had slipped surreptitiously out of the Marten's cottage, she had been plagued by misgivings. No matter how plausible the young squire had been whenever she had seen him, Anne Marten could not rid herself of the thought that everything was not right. Maybe it was because she was still young enough herself to know how things should be between a man and a woman who had gone off to get married, but there was just something in the protracted stories that Corder had subsequently told about their stay in Ipswich - and Maria's failure to write - coupled with their rather strange marriage in London and subsequent retreat so that 'nobody may form the least idea of our residence' that did not add up.

It vexed her, and even when her husband Thomas told her she was worrying over nothing, and should leave the couple to their own lives now they were married, thoughts about them crept unbidden into both her consciousness ... and subconsciousness.

63

Anne Marten   Thomas Marten

On occasions, Anne Marten would gossip with her neighbours in Polstead that she was becoming convinced "something dreadful must have happened to our Maria", and although few were inclined to give more than passing acknowledgement to this, the continuing absence of William Corder and the lack of information as to his whereabouts did give rise to somewhat more concern. It was known that he had not answered any letters since before Christmas, and although no-one seemed inclined to ask old Mrs. Corder for news of her favourite son, one of the servants at the farm said that nothing had been heard from Master William for some months. He seemed, this old man said, to have completely disappeared from the face of the earth.

Throughout that winter of 1827-8, Mrs. Marten had a number of restless nights which sometimes disturbed her husband, though she was at a loss to explain them. Even the children became aware of her tossing and turning in her bed and giving occasional strange cries. Ann, Thomas Marten's daughter by his first marriage, became quite upset by these occurrences and was reported to have said of her stepmother, "She's going queer. Keeps saying Maria comes to her in the night, a-knocking on the door and shouting for help. She ought to be put away."

Thomas Marten knew only too well that there was little love lost between his stepdaughter and his new wife and was therefore inclined to turn a deaf ear to such alarmist reports. But then came the day in early April when Anne Marten could no longer hide the import of her dreams from her husband.

"I have been having the most terrible nightmares about Maria recently," she told him as they ate their frugal breakfast. "I have dreamt on three nights that she was murdered and buried in the Red Barn."

A look of amazement and incredulity spread across the old mole catcher's face as Mrs. Marten went on, "The dream was so real I *know* it must have happened. Go and look in Corder's barn, Thomas, underneath the further bay in the right hand corner."

When he had recovered from his initial shock, Marten began to question his wife more closely about her dream. But he soon found nothing would shake her from her conviction, and even his protestations that her mind was wandering a bit because she had been losing sleep had no effect.

"You must go and look - take someone with you if you will not go alone," she implored him.

Such was the glare of conviction in his wife's eyes, that Thomas Marten knew in that moment he would get no peace until he went to the Red

Anne Marten's nightmare - William Corder murdering her step-daughter and hiding her body in the Red Barn.

A drawing made of the inside of the Red Barn where Maria Marten's body was discovered by her father.

Barn and proved to her that she was only dreaming. So, somewhat embarrassed, he went to see an old friend, Pryke, who worked for the Corders, and asked if he could have a look around the Red Barn. His reason, he said, was that he believed his daughter might have left some clothes there before going off. Although the farm-worker was understandably somewhat puzzled by the request, he agreed to go along with Marten.

What the two men then found in the barn has been described in a halting, but undeniably dramatic, statement which Thomas Marten later made in court:

"I searched the Red Barn on the 19th of April last. In the front of the barn there is a yard, and there are buildings running down on each side, and a little building turning in front; there is also a gate about five or six feet high, or it may be higher. When I went into the barn the bays were covered with litter and fodder. Mrs. Corder's bailiff was in before me; his name is William Pryke.

"We began to poke down in the straw to see if we could find anything, and after trying that way and finding the straw thick, we removed it with a rake, and found some great stones. This was in the

66

middle of the right hand bay, and on account of the stones being up, I thought the earth had been disturbed. I poked down the earth with the handle of a rake and with a mole spike that I had with me; we spiked down these two things, both of us, and turned up something that was black, and pieces of something like flesh stuck to the spike. And I smelled it, and thought it was flesh.

"We were, both of us, struck on seeing this, and we waited to get somebody else; the mole spike was iron, about a foot long, and round. Pryke went to fetch someone and he locked the door and took the key with him. I remained near the barn; this was on a Saturday; Pryke returned, and I, and Wm. Bowtell, and Pryke went into the barn; and we cleared part of the earth away, till we came to a body.

"We cleared towards the head part, and there we found a handkerchief, which appeared to be tied round the neck. We left the handkerchief as we found it, except we raised part of it to see the colour; it was placed two or three times round the neck, and appeared to be tight. We cleared the earth from towards the feet; the body was lying down, but not stretched out; it was about three feet and a half; the legs were bent up, and the head was bent down a little in the earth. A spike was driven into the body about the hip bone; the smallest end of the spike was about the size of my little finger, and increased in thickness till it was more than an inch in diameter.

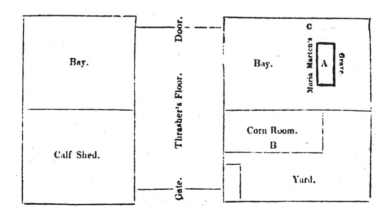

A diagram of the layout of the Red Barn

"I went away and left Pryke and Bowtell there, and returned to them in half an hour, in company with other persons. When I had gone away we had not gone so far as to find her shoes, but they had found them by the time I returned. Mr. Whitmore came with me to the barn, and he advised me to let the body alone till the coroner came, and we did so.

"The coroner came next day and I went with him to the barn, and Mr. Lawton, the surgeon, was there; the body was in the hole in the same state as when I left it on Saturday. The surgeon had a door placed under the body, and it was raised up and brought to the light. I could not tell the body, but I thought when they turned the body up it was like the mouth of my daughter, Maria Marten."

So Anne Marten had been right! In one of the most curious of all cases of premonition - a dream still unique in the annals of crime - she had had a vision of the precise location where the body of her murdered stepdaughter lay. And there could be little doubt that she *had* been murdered.

Remarkable as this discovery was, what has always struck me as even more remarkable about Thomas Marten's description of the body is his statement that a spike had been "driven into the body about the hip bone". To those who know anything about the folklore of the supernatural, an iron spike through a corpse is the traditional method of ensuring that a person suspected of being of evil character, especially a vampire, is prevented from

The staked skeleton of a suspected witch or vampire photographed in Essex in 1921. The body of Maria was also found with an iron spike through the hip

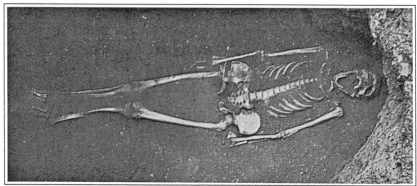

The horrifying discovery of Maria Marten's body in the Red Barn as portrayed in a later Victorian 'penny dreadful'.

rising from their grave after death! Throughout Europe for centuries, the belief has persisted that only by carrying out this gruesome practise at the actual time of burial could people be sure that a member of the undead would not return to drink the blood of the living. In Britain, there are also instances of this impalement being used on the bodies of suspected witches.

I have never come across any suggestion that William Corder believed in vampires or witchcraft - or even that Maria Marten might have been a vampire or witch, though she was undoubtedly a femme fatale - but the strangeness of this discovery still puzzles me, and I am surprised that no-one else appears to have noticed or commented upon it. If there was a sinister reason for Maria being pinned to the earth with that spike, though, I am afraid we shall probably never know what it was after all these years.

Word of the discovery in the Red Barn flew around Polstead and the neighbouring district like wildfire, and even before the local coroner, John Wayman, had arrived to hold an inquest early the very next morning, Sunday, dozens of curious folk had tramped up to the barn to peer in at the grisly scene.

The shock of the discovery had made Anne Marten so ill she was not able to go and confirm the identification of the corpse, but as soon as she was shown the items of clothing taken from the body she was in no doubt it was her stepdaughter. In particular she remembered the handkerchief which was around the girl's neck when she had left the cottage disguised in men's clothes - a silk handkerchief of yellow flowers against a red background. Thomas Marten had also braced himself once more to look at the decomposed and mouldering features of the corpse and knew his first reaction had been correct, all the more so when he noticed the peculiar goitre on the front of the neck which he knew had bothered Maria for years. Just near this he also saw a flesh wound that looked as if it had been inflicted by a knife.

An examination of the barn by the coroner revealed partially-obliterated bloodstains on the floor and the marks of bullets on one of the doors. To Mr. Wayman it seemed patently obvious that Maria Marten had been murdered and her body then hastily buried in a shallow grave. What was puzzling was whether she had been shot, stabbed or possibly even strangled by the handkerchief tied tightly around her neck.

Although the coroner closed his inquest without any reference as to who might have committed such a terrible crime, local gossip was already busy on that score. And for the people of Polstead there was only one possible suspect - the missing William Corder.

Wasn't he the last person to have been seen with Maria, they said, and hadn't he gone off so that nobody knew where he was? If further proof was needed, hadn't William Pryke, his bailiff, declared that Corder insisted the Red Barn was always kept locked and only opened on his instructions? That was until that fateful morning when he and Thomas Marten had made their entry.

What the coroner, John Wayman, had ordered was for further enquiries to be made, and the local police constable, John Balham, was in no doubt that his first objective was to trace the absent Squire of Corder's Farm. Knowing his suspect's predilection for visiting London, he straightaway directed his attentions to the metropolis, enlisting the aid of an astute detective from Lambeth Police Station, named James Lea. A man with considerable knowledge of London and its underworld, he was not long in tracking down Corder to Ealing and, armed with a warrant for his arrest, confronted him about the murder of Maria.

The Sunday Times of April 27, 1828 - the self-same paper in which Corder had advertised for a wife - takes up the story of what happened next:

The intrepid detective, James Lea, who tracked down William Corder.

71

The Arrest of Corder.

James Lea arresting Corder in London as the fugitive is about to start his breakfast.

'With a loose clue, afforded by the country constable, Lea traced the prisoner, first to Gray's Inn Terrace, and from thence, through a number of intermediate places, to his residence in Ealing-lane, Brentford, where he apprehended him. A stratagem was necessary to obtain an entrance, and he procured it by representing that he had a daughter whom he was anxious to place under the care of his wife. On going in, he found him in the parlour with two ladies, at breakfast. He was in his dressing-gown, and had a watch before him, by which he was minuting the boiling of some eggs. Lea called him on one side, and told him that he was a police officer, and had to apprehend him on a most serious charge. He seemed alarmed, and, at his request, they retired into the drawing-room; but, on his being made acquainted with the nature of the offence, he denied all knowledge of it. Also of his unfortunate victim. Lea, after having secured him, proceeded to search both his person and drawers, and discovered a number of letters. He also found a case of detonating pocket pistols, maker's name 'Harcourt, Ipswich,' supposed to have been purchased on the day of the murder, together with a powder-flask, and a quantity of balls.'

It was the work of only hours for Lea to have Corder formally charged and committed in custody to be taken back to Polstead. This done, he handed him over to another Polstead constable named Ayres to be transported to Suffolk.

By the time the coach in which Corder was riding had reached Colchester on Wednesday evening, word of his arrest and return to stand trial had reached Essex and "immense crowds were collected to see him", according to one account. Some reports of his journey state that "the prisoner conducted himself with astonishing levity, and disgusted every person on the roof of the coach", but others are equally adamant that he was quiet and reserved through the 50-mile journey. At Colchester, he was kept overnight at the 'George Inn' and there wrote a most revealing letter to his mother in Polstead, which has survived in facsimile and is reproduced on page 60.

The following day the crowds grew still larger around the inn, while inside Corder paced his room restlessly, muttering on several occasions, "Oh, if I could be as free from sin as my beloved wife." Such indeed was the concourse of people in the town, that it was decided Corder could only be moved safely to Polstead under cover of darkness, and consequently he was secreted away by coach just before midnight, arriving at the Cock Inn at two o'clock.

Later that same day, Corder appeared briefly before Coroner John Wayman. Somewhat perversely Wayman denied the press reporting facilities on a technicality of the law, saying that they would have to await the trial to gather specific details. The jury then heard the outline of the case against Corder and swiftly brought in a verdict of "wilful murder", committing the prisoner for trial at Bury St. Edmunds. Of Corder's demeanour at this moment, one newspaperman wrote, "The unhappy man is but 24. He presented a most melancholy object. His head reclined on his shoulder, and he appeared unconscious of what was going on."

No time was lost in transporting Corder by postchaise to Bury - but legend has ever been busy with this seemingly straightforward aspect of our story. For according to a tale which persists in nearby Boxford, where I live, the journey of the suspected murderer was broken in this village, where he dined in the upstairs room of The Fleece Hotel - to avoid the stares of curiosity-seekers, according to gossip - and was then incarcerated overnight in the small jail just across the road beside the River Box.

I am sorry to say that while both The Fleece and the jail still exist today (the hotel even naming one of its rooms "The Corder Room", while the little prison now serves as a bus shelter), and it is a fact that Corder did in all probability pass through Boxford on his way to Bury, there is no evidence whatsoever to support the claim he stayed there overnight. In truth, with all the public clamour growing around the prisoner, the authorities were undoubtedly most anxious to get him safely behind bars for their peace of mind as well as his own safety!

Once Corder was safely installed in Bury St. Edmunds Jail his wife, Mary, was allowed to visit him, and although she was clearly shattered at what had been alleged against the man she had known for such a short while, she still showed herself devoted to him. Indeed, right through the trial and after his sentence, she remained unswervingly loyal at the cost of both her reputation and the closing of her boarding school. To add to her troubles, the poor woman also discovered that she was pregnant.

Corder, for his part, was obviously deeply distressed at what his wife was undergoing at this time, and his letters to her constantly mention how heartbroken he is over what has happened and how he worries for her future. He only has his religion to comfort him, he says, as he realises, "I must soon depart from this vale of misery."

* * *

The summer months between May and August dragged agonisingly slowly for William Corder in Bury St. Edmunds Jail while the counsels for the prosecution and defence prepared their cases. His wife Mary continued to visit him regularly, secured what she hoped would be a good lawyer for his defence and brought him news of the outside world. What she could not bring herself to tell him, though, was that the body of Maria Marten had finally been laid to rest on April 20 in the pretty little church of St. Mary's on the top of the hill in Polstead, the funeral being attended by the Marten family and literally hundreds of inquisitive sightseers. Already, it was clear, interest in the affair was growing at a pace.

When the case finally came into court in the Shire Hall, Bury St. Edmunds, on the morning of Thursday, August 7, the place was - to quote one newspaper - "crowded to suffocation", people having queued in the rain since before six o'clock. For days men and women had been assembling in the town from all over East Anglia, clamouring for a place to hear a case they suspected was going to make legal history. This became evident immediately after Corder had taken his place in the dock before Chief Baron Alexander and the jurors, and the clerk had read out no less than ten charges against the accused. *The Sunday Times* reports thus:

> "Mr. Edgell, the clerk of the arraigns, read the indictment, which consisted of ten counts. They charged that the prisoner had mortally wounded the deceased with a pistol shot, that he had stabbed her with a sharp instrument between the fifth and sixth rib, that he had wounded her with a sword on the right side of her face, and also on the right side of her neck, and that he had choked and strangled her with a handkerchief, and that he had suffocated her, by throwing large quantities of earth on her, in a hole in the Red Barn. The pistol, sword, handkerchief, and hole are described in the usual phraseology of the law.
> "When the learned gentleman had concluded, he said to Corder - 'William Corder, are you Guilty of the murder of Maria Marten, or Not Guilty?' - Corder: 'Not Guilty, My Lord.' "

Through the long, hot hours of that day and on into Friday the members of Maria Marten's family, her father and stepmother, her sister Ann and brother George, a number of Polstead villagers including William Pryke who had helped find the body, Maria's one-time lover Peter Mathews, the eagle-eyed police officer, James Lea, and various medical experts followed each other one by one into the witness box to relate their parts in the story of the murder in the Red Barn. The packed public gallery listened with bated breath as the case built up inexorably against Corder, while in the press enclosure the pens of the journalists took down every word for their thousands of eagerly-awaiting readers.

The prosecution's star witness was Anne Marten, Maria's stepmother, on whose testimony much of the case against Corder had been built and whose words, indeed, were responsible for a considerable part of the Red Barn legend. In her statement to the court she talked of her stepdaughter's promiscuous lifestyle in painstaking detail, and also demonstrated an exceptional recall of conversations which had apparently taken place during the final hours before Maria had disappeared with Corder.

Describing that last fateful Friday, Anne Marten told the packed courtroom how she had helped Maria to dress in the male clothing and then watched as the pair had left her house. Mrs. Marten's account then went on most specifically.

"I saw that Corder had a gun with him when he went away," she said. "And in reply to my question, 'Is that gun loaded?' he said, 'Yes' and he added, 'I'll move it away on account of the child' (Maria's son, Thomas Henry.) After this they went away across Harehill Field in the direction of the Red Barn. I saw neither of them afterwards that day, and have not seen Maria since."

On the following Monday, though, Mrs. Marten continued, she did see Corder again in Polstead. "I said to him, 'William, what have you done with Maria?' He said, 'I have left her at Ipswich. I have got her a comfortable place; she is going down with Miss Rowley to the water side.' I said, 'William, what will she do for clothes?' and he said, 'Miss Rowley has got plenty and would not let me send for any.' He then added, 'I have got a licence, but it must go to London to be signed and I can't marry until a month or six weeks.' I asked which way they went to Ipswich and he said by Stratford. I then said, 'Where did she dress?' and he replied, 'She put her things on at the barn, and put the great coat over them to hide her till we could get into a carriage for our journey to Ipswich.' "

Mrs. Marten added that she had not seen the body of her step-daughter following its discovery in the barn, although she had identified those items of clothing from the corpse which had been brought for her inspection.

"I was ill at the time," she concluded, seeming to stifle a sob. "My husband and I had been afraid for some time that Maria might be taken up. The last thing I saw when she went away on the 18th was that she was crying."

If Mrs. Marten's testimony moved the judge and jury - as it evidently did - it was also lacking in one singular aspect. For not once during her evidence or cross-examination did she make any mention of her extraordinary dream which was supposed to have set the whole chain of events into motion.

Interest was at fever pitch by the Friday afternoon when Corder was finally called to the witness box to give for the first time his side of the story. Such had been the press of people trying to get into the court following the lunch recess, that Chief Baron Alexander had actually been pushed off his feet and a way for him and the lawyers had had to be cleared by court officials holding long wooden staves.

Although the full transcript of Corder's testimony is long, and often repetitive, the heart of his defence is worth reprinting in full, I think, particularly because we have it in his own words. After first imploring the judge and jury in a "feeble and tremulous tone" to put from their minds all the sensational and inaccurate stories that had been alleged against him and which prejudiced his case, he asked everyone to "listen to my true and simple detail of the real facts of the death of this unfortunate woman." Then he went on.

"At first I gave a false account of the death of the unfortunate Maria. I am now resolved to disclose the truth, regardless of the consequences. To conceal her pregnancy from my mother, I took lodgings at Sudbury: she was delivered of a female child, which died in a fortnight in the arms of Mrs. Marten, although the newspapers have so perverted the fact; and it was agreed between Mrs. Marten, Maria, and me, that the child should be buried in the fields. There was a pair of small pistols in the bedroom; Maria knew they were there. I had often showed them to her. Maria took them away from me. I had some reason to suspect she had some correspondence with a gentleman, by whom she had a child, in London. Though her conduct was not free from blemish, I at length yielded to her entreaties and agreed to marry her, and it was arranged we should go to Ipswich, and procure a licence and marry. Whether I said there was a warrant out against her I know not. It has been proved that we had many words, and she was crying when she left the house.

"Gentlemen - This was the origin of the fatal occurrence. As we proceeded across the fields to the barn (which I beg you to bear in mind was a place where we were in the constant habit of meeting and passing hours together, and even nights together), I gently reproved her for giving away to tears, and observed to her, that that was not the way she should conduct herself towards one who was willing to make her happy. By this time we had reached the barn, when in consequence of this and other observations which I passed, and whilst she was changing her dress, she flew into a passion; told me that she did not care anything about me, that I was too proud to take

William Corder sketched in Bury Jail as he awaits his trial for murder in the summer of 1828

her to my mother's, and when married she did not think she should be happy, as my mother and family she was sure would never notice her. She upbraided me with not having so much regard for her as the gentleman before alluded to had shown. Much further conversation arose, the particulars of which it is useless to detail, but I felt myself so insulted, and became so much irritated by her observations, that I told her if she would go on in this way before we were married, what could I expect afterwards; that I had then seen sufficient to convince me we should never live happily together, and I was, therefore, resolved, before it was too late, not to marry her, informing her that I should return home, and that she might act as she thought proper respecting her future conduct. In consequence of this determination, I turned from her, and had scarcely proceeded to the outer gate of the barn-yard, when I heard a loud report like that of a gun or pistol. Alarmed at this noise, I immediately ran back, and to my horror I found the unhappy girl on the ground apparently dead. Astonished at the suddenness of the occurrence, and overwhelmed by my own feelings at the awful event, I stood for some moments in a state of complete stupefaction. When I had in some measure recovered from this stupor, my first thought was to run for assistance, and well had it been for me had I acted on that impulse; but the dreadful situation of Maria deterred me from quitting the spot. I endeavoured to raise her from the ground in the hope of affording her relief, but to my horror I found she was altogether lifeless. I then placed the body on the ground, in doing which I perceived the fatal weapon, which I took up, when, to add to my terror, and the extraordinary singularity of my situation, I discovered it to be one of my own pistols, which I had always kept loaded in my bed-room. The danger of my situation now flashed upon my mind. There lay the unfortunate girl wounded to death, and by an instrument belonging to me, and I the only human being present who could prove how the circumstance occurred. I will not attempt to describe to you (because it would be impossible) the agitation of my mind at finding myself surrounded by such suspicious and unfortunate circumstances. My faculties for the time seemed suspended. I knew not what to do, and some time elapsed before I sufficiently recovered myself to become thoroughly sensible of the awful and responsible situation in which I stood.

The instant the mischief happened, I thought to have made it public: but this would have added to the suspicion, and I resolved to conceal her death. I then buried her in the best way I could. I tried to conceal the fact as well as I could, giving sometimes one reason for her absence, and sometimes another. It may be said, why not prove all this by witnesses? Alas! how can I?"

It was an impassioned speech, given in a voice filled with emotion, and left the whole courtroom silent for some moments after it had ended. Corder sat down slowly and did not look up again until Chief Barn Alexander began to deliver his closing remarks. In a reasonable summing-up of the evidence, although he admitted he found the case against the accused formidable, and his explanation unconvincing, he instructed the jury that if they had any sort of doubt about William Corder being the murderer of Maria Marten then they must give him the benefit of the doubt. If not, then they should without fear of the consequences bring in a verdict of guilty against him.

The jury were absent from the courtroom for just thirty-five minutes before returning. And in a quiet voice the foreman announced that they had to a man found William Corder guilty of the crime of murdering Maria Marten.

On hearing the verdict, a newspaper said, "Corder raised his hand slowly to his forehead, pressed it for a moment, and then dropped it most dejectedly. His head immediately fell drooping on his bosom. During the passing of the sentence, his firmness still continued in some degree, but at the close of it he sobbed loudly and convulsively for some moments."

After asking Corder if he had anything further to say and receiving no reply, the judge pronounced the sentence of hanging and added finally: "You sent this unfortunate woman to her account without giving her time for preparation. She had no time to turn her eyes to the Throne of Grace for mercy and for forgiveness. She had no opportunity given to her to repent of her many transgressions. The same measure is not meted out to you: a small interval is allowed you for preparation. Use it well, for the scene of this world closes upon you; but another and, I hope, a better world is opening for you."

Whether the dazed and trembling Corder was conscious of these words of comfort as he was led from the dock and back to his cell in the prison there is no way of knowing. What he could not help being aware of was that his time was running out. He had only the weekend, until Monday morning, in fact, before he was to be hanged.

But even in that short time, those precious forty-eight hours, he probably became aware that a legend was already being created around him, Maria Marten, and the murder in the Red Barn, which would last long after each and every one of them had crumbled to dust . . .

6

A Legend is Born . . . and Still Continues

* * *

"FROM AN EARLY hour in the morning, the population of the surrounding districts came pouring into Bury; and the whole of the labouring classes in that town struck work for the day, in order that they might have an opportunity of witnessing the execution of this wretched criminal, which was appointed to take place at 12 o'clock noon. As early as 9 o'clock in the morning upwards of 1,000 persons were assembled around the scaffold, in the paddock on the south side of the jail, and their numbers kept increasing till 12 o'clock, when they amounted to at least 7,000 persons."

Such was the way in which *The Sunday Times* of August 17, 1828 described the scene outside Bury St. Edmunds Jail on the morning of William Corder's execution, Monday August 11, 1828. Some estimates of the crowd put the number much higher at almost 20,000, but what remains indisputable is that there was tremendous interest in the last moments of this now infamous man.

Rumour had already got to work on the story and was embellishing some of the more unsavoury aspects of the case, while those who make profit from other's misfortunes were busy parting the sensation-hungry public from their hard-earned cash. As we have heard during the trial, there had been a good deal of comment on the murder in the press - much of it embellished and highly inaccurate to sell more newspapers - and on fairgrounds and public places throughout southern England showmen were exhibiting peep shows and models of the killing as they imagined it to have happened in the Red Barn. In some of these displays Maria was already being shown as the village maiden cruelly wronged, and her murderer as a heartless man of rank willing to kill rather than accept his responsibility for having taken her good name. Historian H.G.Hibbert in his book *A Playgoer's Memories* (1920) tells us that one of these peep shows at

The enormous crowd which gathered outside Bury Jail for Corder's hanging.

Polstead Fair "founded the fortune of Lord George Sanger" while at the famous Bartholomew Fair that same year "a hundred pounds was taken in a booth exhibiting 'Corder's Head' - a plaster cast no doubt!"

Lord George Sanger, the famous showman, was actually a small boy at the time, travelling with his father, the creator of a primitive peep-show which he set up and operated for view wherever there might be a paying audience. Years later, Sanger was to recall in his biography, *Seventy Years a Showman* (1926):

> "It was my task to proclaim the attractions of father's show. 'Walk up!' I would pipe, 'Walk up and see the only correct views of the terrible murder of Maria Marten. They are historically accurate and true to life, depicting the death of Maria at the hands of the villain Corder in the famous Red Barn. You will see how the ghost of Maria appeared to her mother on three successive nights at the bedside, leading to the discovery of the body and the arrest of Corder at Eveley Grove House, Brentford, seven miles from London.

You will actually see the arrest of the murderer Corder as he was at breakfast with the two Miss Singletons. Lea, the officer, is seen entering the door and telling Corder of the serious charge against him. Observe the horrified faces, and note also, so true to life are the pictures, that even the saucepan is shown upon the fire and the minute glass upon the table timing the boiling of the eggs! Walk up! Walk up! - and view the most appalling crime of the century!"

The judge at the trial, Chief Baron Alexander, had had a few words to say about such displays, and his views were probably shared by other responsible people. But, seemingly, no-one was prepared to do anything about stopping them. "We have been told," he said, "that drawings and placards have been dispersed, not only in the neighbourhood of this town, but also in the immediate vicinity of the hall in which the trial is taking place, tending to manifest detriment of the prisoner at the bar. Such a practice is so indecorous and unjust that I can with difficulty bring myself to believe that any person, even in the very lowest class, will so far degrade himself as to think of deriving gain from the exhibition of this melancholy transaction."

But such people there certainly were, and in addition even a number of clergymen and preachers who had latched on to the story as being ideal material for the most inflammatory sermons. These 'Hell Fire Gospellers' adapted and distorted the facts to suit their own particular ends, and used the story as a perfect example of the price that had to be paid for sins of the flesh.

The most popular items with the public, though, were undoubtedly the broadsheets which detailed the most sensational incidents of the trial and were hurried from the press to street sellers within hours of each hearing. The most famous publisher of these items at the time was James Catnach (1792-1841), a London printer based in Seven Dials who published single page sheets - each selling for a penny - on subjects ranging from notorious criminal cases to society scandals, duels, assassinations, robberies, sudden deaths, suicides and all manner of dark deeds. These publications, which earned the nick-name of 'catch pennies' were as full of fiction as fact, and where 'Jemmy' Catnach could not obtain the facts, he just made them up. He published two broadsheets on the Red Barn murder - the first immediately after the discovery of Maria's body, (which is reprinted in the Appendix to this book) and the second following the arrest of Corder. But it was his publication of the 'Last Speech and Dying Confession' of the murderer that brought him the greatest financial reward. Catnach had long made a speciality of such confessions both genuine and spurious, but none enjoyed quite the success of the item reprinted in facsimile here. In the days following the execution it is estimated that 1,166,000 copies of the broadsheet were sold! As a matter of interest, the "lamentable verses" attributed to "W.Corder" were in all probability written by 'Jemmy' himself!

During the course of the weekend since he had been brought back to the jail from the Shire Hall, Corder had, apart from having a last tearful re-union with his wife, been under almost constant pressure from the two prison chaplains to confess his crime so that he could go to his death with a clear conscience. Also encouraging him to confess was the governor of the jail, John Orridge, who, as soon as Corder had finally succumbed to their urging, witnessed the document and then hurried a copy out to the waiting pressmen. Even before the sun was properly up on the Monday morning, the words were in print and being hawked in the streets of London, Ipswich, Sudbury and, of course, Bury St. Edmunds.

John Orridge, the governor of Bury Jail, who urged Corder to confess his guilt.

CONFESSION AND EXECUTION OF
WILLIAM CORDER,
THE MURDERER OF MARIA MARTEN.

Since the tragical affair between Thurtell and Weare, no event has occurred connected with the criminal annals of our country which has excited so much interest as the trial of Corder, who was justly convicted of the murder of Maria Marten on Friday last.

THE CONFESSION.

"Bury Gaol, August 10th, 1828.—Condemned cell.
"Sunday evening, half-past Eleven.

"I acknowledge being guilty of the death of poor Maria Marten, by shooting her with a pistol. The particulars are as follows:—When we left her father's house, we began quarrelling about the burial of the child: she apprehended the place wherein it was deposited would be found out. The quarrel continued about three quarters of an hour upon this sad and about other subjects. A scuffle ensued, and during the scuffle, and at the time I think that she had hold of me, I took the pistol from the side pocket of my velveteen jacket and fired. She fell, and died in an instant. I never saw her even struggle. I was overwhelmed with agitation and dismay:—the body fell near the front doors on the floor of the barn. A vast quantity of blood issued from the wound, and ran on to the floor and through the crevices. Having determined to bury the body in the barn (about two hours after she was dead. I went and borrowed a spade of Mrs Stow, but before I went there I dragged the body from the barn into the chaff-house, and looked the barn. I returned again to the barn, and began to dig a hole, but the spade being a bad one, and the earth firm and hard, I was obliged to go home for a pickaxe and a better spade, with which I dug the hole, and then buried the body. I think I dragged the body by the handkerchief that was tied round her neck. It was dark when I finished covering up the body. I went the next day, and washed the blood from off the barn-floor. I declare to Almighty God I had no sharp instrument about me, and no other wound but the one made by the pistol was inflicted by me. I have been guilty of great idleness, and at times led a dissolute life, but I hope through the mercy of God to be forgiven. WILLIAM CORDER."

Witness to the signing by the said William Corder,
JOHN ORRIDGE.

Condemned cell, Eleven o'clock, Monday morning,
August 11th, 1828.

The above confession was read over carefully to the prisoner in our presence, who stated most solemnly it was true, and that he had nothing to add to or retract from it.—W. STOCKING, chaplain; TIMOTHY R. HOLMES, Under-Sheriff.

THE EXECUTION.

At ten minutes before twelve o'clock the prisoner was brought from his cell and pinioned by the hangman, who was brought from London for the purpose. He appeared resigned, but was so weak as to be unable to stand without support; when his cravat was removed he groaned heavily, and appeared to be labouring under great mental agony. When his wrists and arms were made fast, he was led round towards the scaffold, and

as he passed the different yards in which the prisoners were confined, he shook hands with them, and speaking to two of them by name, he said, "Good bye, God bless you." They appeared considerably affected by the wretched appearance which he made, and "God bless you!" "May God receive your soul!" were frequently uttered as he passed along. The chaplain walked before the prisoner, reading the usual Burial Service, and the Governor and Officers walking immediately after him. The prisoner was supported to the steps which led to the scaffold; he looked somewhat wildly around, and a constable was obliged to support him while the hangman was adjusting the fatal cord. There was a barrier to keep off the crowd, amounting to upwards of 7,000 persons, who at this time had stationed themselves in the adjoining fields, on the hedges, the tops of houses, and at every point from which a view of the execution could be best obtained. The prisoner, a few moments before the drop fell, groaned heavily, and would have fallen, had not a second constable caught hold of him. Everything having been made ready, the signal was given, the fatal drop fell, and the unfortunate man was launched into eternity. Just before he was turned off, he said in a feeble tone, "I am justly sentenced, and may God forgive me"

The Murder of Maria Marten.
BY W. CORDER

COME all you thoughtless young men, a warning take by me,
And think upon my unhappy fate to be hanged upon a tree;
My name is William Corder, to you I do declare,
I courted Maria Marten, most beautiful and fair.

I promised I would marry her upon a certain day,
Instead of that, I was resolved to take her life away.
I went into her father's house the 18th day of May,
Saying, my dear Maria, we will fix the wedding day.

If you will meet me at the Red-barn, as sure as I have life,
I will take you to Ipswich town, and there make you my wife;
I then went home and fetched my gun, my pickaxe and my spade,
I went into the Red-barn, and there I dug her grave.

With heart so light, she thought no harm, to meet him she did go
He murdered her all in the barn, and laid her body low;
After the horrible deed was done, she lay weltering in her gore,
Her bleeding mangled body he buried beneath the Red-barn floor.

Now all things being silent, her spirit could not rest,
She appeared unto her mother, who suckled her at her breast,
For many a long month or more, her mind being sore oppress'd,
Neither night or day she could not take any rest.

Her mother's mind being so disturbed, she dreamt three nights o'er,
Her daughter she lay murdered beneath the Red-barn floor;
She sent the father to the barn, when he the ground did thrust,
And there he found his daughter mingling with the dust.

My trial is hard, I could not stand, most woeful was the sight,
When her jaw-bone was brought to prove, which pierced my heart quite;
Her aged father standing by, likewise his loving wife,
And in her grief her hair she tore, she scarcely could keep life.

Adieu, adieu, my loving friends, my glass is almost run,
On Monday next will be my last, when I am to be hang'd;
So you, young men, who do pass by, with pity look on me,
For murdering Maria Marten, I was hang'd upon the tree.

Printed by J. Catnach, 2 and 3, Monmouth Court.—Cards, &c., Printed Cheap.

One of James Catnach's famous penny broadsheets complete with Corder's alleged 'Confession' and a piece of verse he is said to have written in the condemned cell!

By this statement Corder had seemingly recanted his story that Maria had killed herself, and if anyone nursed the slightest doubt about his innocence this seemed to put an end to such speculation. Even further damning evidence was contained in his last speech, according to James Catnach's broadsheet when it appeared a few hours after the execution. As the reader can see from the facsimile the sheet also has a blow by blow account of the last moment of Corder's life on the gallows.

Strangely, for Catnach was not a man to shy away from grisly details, he did not include (or more likely did not know about) the difficulty with which Corder died. However, *The Sunday Times* reporter in the issue of August 17 spares us nothing of what happened when the platform beneath the noose fell:

"The executioner seized him by the knees, and held him for some time while he struggled in the agonies of death. He held him for about two minutes in this way, when all suffering appeared to be over, though fully ten minutes afterwards a cunvulsive movement was observed. The body was left hanging for an hour, then cut down, and taken in a cart with a little straw to the Shire Hall, where it was exhibited and seen by 5,000 people filing past . . . It is also an extraordinary fact, and certainly not to be accounted for on any principle of reason or common sense, that the rope with which Corder was hanged has become an article of arduous competition. I have been informed that it has been sold for a guinea an inch to the various parties who bade for it!"

There was quite a struggle among several law officers to secure Corder's two pistols and knife: Police Officer James Lea maintaining the dead man had promised them to him, while the Prison Governor, John Orridge, said they were now the property of the State. After passing through several hands, the items finally came to rest at Moyse's Hall Museum in Bury St. Edmunds where they are now on permanent display with a plaster death mask of Corder's face made shortly after the execution and the account of his life and trial bound in human skin.

From such incidents it was clearly becoming evident that here was a case that had caught the public imagination like no other in recent memory - and interest in it was not going to die with Corder's death. Indeed, it was going to grow and multiply with each passing month and year.

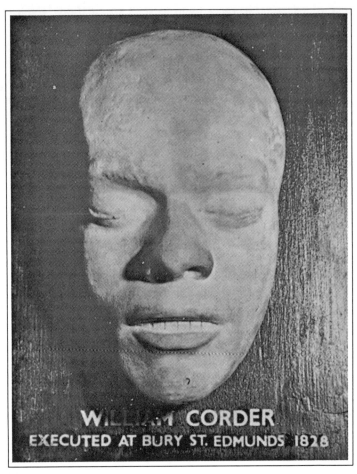

William Corder's plaster death mask made shortly after his execution on the gallows in Bury Jail.

The pair of pistols allegedly used by Corder to murder Maria Marten which both John Orridge and James Lea claimed.

The newspapers naturally had a field day with the murder trial, as did the magazines and periodicals, the more enterprising vying with each other to print "faithful representations" of the locality and leading personalities - some of which are reproduced in the pages of this book. Pictures of the deceased Maria portrayed her as anything from a rather vacant-looking country girl to an out-and-out trollop. And William Corder, while he was still alive, fared no better at the hands of these artists. Such was the scramble among newspapermen to get a portrait of Corder into their columns, that the most absurd things happened as in the following example cited in Charles Hindley's book *The Life and Times of James Catnach* (1878):

"An artist had been sent from Ipswich to sketch a portrait of Corder for one of the newspapers of that town; but the sketcher mistook a journalist named Curtis for Corder, and in the next number of the journal Mr. Curtis figured in full length as the murderer of Maria Marten. He bore the mistake with good humour, and regarded this as one of the most amusing incidents of his life."

This man James Curtis is also an interesting figure in our story in that he is credited with having published the first book on the murder in the Red Barn which appeared a month or so after Corder's execution. Curtis was employed as a reporter by *The Times* and was dispatched to Suffolk to cover the case immediately after the arrest of Corder. It was the kind of assignment he relished, as Charles Hindley has told us:

"Curtis was an eccentric person whose taste for witnessing executions and for the society of persons sentenced to death was remarkable. He had been present at every execution in the metropolis and its neighbourhood for the last quarter of a century."

The writer James Curtis who published the first book on the murder in the Red Barn and was mistaken for Corder himself by one artist sent to depict the trial.

Curtis would apparently walk many miles to be the first on the scene of a crime, and shared the last hours of a number of notorious criminals in Newgate Prison. According to Hindley he was the first reporter to see Corder after his arrest, and during the ensuing weeks struck up something akin to a friendship with him. This may well account for his being confused with Corder by the artist from Ipswich.

In any event, Curtis provided columns of text for *The Times*, and then immediately after the execution reworked the material into book form, adding his own comments and interpretations on much that had happened.

The book was published by a London printer, Thomas Kelly (who later became Lord Mayor of London in 1837-8), under the somewhat pretentious title of *An Authentic & Faithful History of the Mysterious Murder of Maria Marten*. Not surprisingly, the book was an immediate best-seller, and some of Curtis' prejudice against Corder and misplaced sympathy for Maria undoubtedly helped in the creation of the popular images of these two people as legend later came to portray them. (It is also a matter of record that it was Curtis' book which was later bound in a piece of skin dissected from Corder's corpse and deposited in a local library as a rather gruesome souvenir).

In some studies of the Murder in the Red Barn, Curtis' book is given all the credit for helping this legend develop, but in my opinion a serial story based on the events which began its publication only a week after the execution was far more influential in the emergence of the melodramatic version of the tale. I believe this view may have developed because of the extreme scarcity of copies of the serial, and indeed of the complete book subsequently published. I should, therefore, like to briefly outline here the details of the book and its plot to justify my claim - beginning, first, with another quote from Charles Hindley's book on Catnach:

"It is not generally known that a Dr. Maginn wrote for Knight and Lacy, the publishers in Paternoster Row, a novel embodying the strange story of the Polstead murder, in 1828, under the title of *The Red Barn*. The work was published anonymously, in numbers, and by its sale the publishers cleared many hundreds of pounds."

One of the reasons why previous writers have probably tended to overlook the influence of this book in the creation of the Maria Marten legend is because its publication date is cited in most authorities (vide *A Gothic Bibliography* by Montague Summers) as 1831, whereas the first edition was published in 1828 and it is from a rare surviving copy belonging to my friend the antiquarian book collector, David Philips, that I have drawn my information.

Although the author's name is not listed, we know that it was written by William Maginn, an ill-fated, often penniless writer who was forced to churn out potboiler novels to eke out his existence. In his *Playgoer's Memories*, H.G.Hibbert confirms this attribution, calling the author "Bright, broken Maginn - Thackeray's Captain Shandon" and adds that "on this novel innumerable plays were based": a point we shall return to later.

What *The Red Barn* does demonstrate was that Maginn was capable of weaving a compelling story against a factual background and it seems evident that he must have obtained considerable 'inside' knowledge of the case before he wrote the book. To this information he coupled his own powers of imagination to produce a novelisation of the events in the Red Barn which, as I said, helped create the legend as we know it today. The book was also enhanced by eight full-page engravings depicting highlights from the story and all of these are reproduced in this volume. Sadly, we know little of the artist beyond his name, R.Seymour, for he shows every indication of having a good knowledge of both his subjects and the localities of the story.

In introducing his 600-page novel, Maginn stresses that it is "a fiction, founded on fact, for the purpose of exhibiting the fatal consequences of loose principles and dissolute habits too frequently contracted by the young and thoughtless in this great metropolis." He adds that "real names are never mentioned, except where no possible harm can result from mentioning them" yet while he has no compunction in presenting Maria Marten and her family under their real names, Corder is disguised as William Barnard, and the old roue Peter Mathews is called Stafford Jackson. Admittedly the disguises are so transparent that no reader of the time (or of today, for that matter) can have been in the slightest doubt as to whom he was referring.

The novel of *The Red Barn* begins by introducing us to Maria Marten - 'a perfect village beauty' - a kind, virtuous and happy young woman of eighteen. The object of much male admiration, she is particularly loved by one young village lad, Harry Everton, who is too shy to profess his feelings, although he is actively encouraged to do so by Maria's gentle, ageing parents. His chances of winning her hand are somewhat diminished, however, when Maria is approached by a beautiful, dark-skinned fortune-teller named Hannah Woods who predicts a glamorous future for her with a rich and handsome young man on horseback whom she will meet at Polstead Fair.

At the fair, Maria does indeed come face to face with this mysterious stranger who attempts to carry her off to his home, but she resists his blandishments although she does admit to wishing to see him again. As she walks home delightedly she meets another man on horseback. "His name was William Barnard. He was a very young man, the son of a rich farmer

92

in the neighbourhood." Barnard has obviously been drinking and he, too, tries to proposition Maria with declarations of love. She breaks away and as she hurries home, begins to wonder which of the two men on horseback the fortune-teller meant she was to marry.

Maginn then switches the scene of his narrative to London to a low dive and introduces us to the first man on horseback that Maria met - Stafford Jackson, gambler, smuggler, drinker and roue. With his unsavoury companion, Jack 'Beauty' Smith, he leads a life of crime and debauchery, cheating, swindling and seducing the innocents of both sex. From time to time he resides in the Polstead area, and it is he who introduces the restless young William Barnard to low-life in the Capital, getting him drunk and helping him to lose £200 at cards. Following this, Barnard returns to his home somewhat chastened, but by no means put off London life.

In the meantime, Maria has been waiting for the man on horseback (Jackson) to reappear and continue courting her, but when he does not materialise she succumbs to the renewed attentions of William Barnard who invites her to go to a dance being held at the Red Barn. A last-minute attempt by the unhappy Harry Everton to dissuade her from going, or having anything to do with Barnard or Stafford Jackson, because of what he has learned of their characters, falls on deaf ears.

At the dance, however, Barnard's eye falls on another woman, Hannah Woods, and the unfortunate Maria can only watch helplessly as her escort is lured away and quickly seduced by the beautiful fortune-teller. At this juncture the reader learns that Hannah is in fact in league with Stafford Jackson in a life of crime and that she plans to help him seduce Maria Marten: first by destroying any regard she may have for Barnard. Once the young landowner's son is hopelessly in love with her, Jackson quickly moves into accomplish Maria's downfall. When, though, she proves rather more determined to hang on to her innocence than he had bargained for, he attempts to kidnap her with the aid of 'Beauty' Smith, but the plan is foiled by the loyal and vigilant Harry Everton.

Frustrated in this objective, Jackson nonetheless manages to encourage the besotted William Barnard to return to London with Hannah, the woman he believes to be his mistress. By so doing he hopes to part Barnard from more of his inheritance, and the foolish young man seems quite incapable of seeing how he is being used by both Jackson and his cohort

Smith. In a short and riotous period of time, they encourage him to sink further and further into debt and show him how to connive increasingly large sums of money out of his unsuspecting father back in Polstead.

After a suitable period has elapsed, Jackson returns to Polstead to try and seduce Maria once again, more gently this time. With skilful blandishments he convinces her it was the heat of love that made him try to carry her off, and he now only wishes to make her his bride. Easily deceived by his manner, the young maiden consents to the request and they are married - but unknown to her the 'priest' is one of Jackson's cronies. Barnard, too, is tricked again and again by his so-called London friends, and when finally his father realises what has been happening he cuts his son off from his inheritance. Jackson then skilfully owns up to the game he has been playing and invites his victim to join them all in a life of crime! Blinded by love for Hannah, whose expensive tastes have also been responsible for draining his resources, he agrees.

But now there is a falling out among the thieves. 'Beauty' Smith inveigles Barnard to join him in some robberies on their own, cutting out Jackson from the spoils: but the plans soon go astray. The young squire also comes face to face with Maria Marten who has soon been abandoned by Jackson once he has had his wicked way with her. And in a further terrible moment of disillusionment he overhears a conversation between Hannah and Stafford Jackson and realises how he, too, has been duped. In a fury of remorse, he decides to return to Polstead with Maria and have nothing more to do with London life.

Perhaps fortuitously for Barnard, his father dies suddenly at this moment and having left no will, his erring son comes into the whole estate. William determines to settle for the life of a country squire, but somehow he cannot quite give up his friendship with 'Beauty' Smith who seems to have been the only one who served him well in London - nor can he banish thoughts of Maria Marten from his mind. Since her return from London and the fraudulent 'marriage' to Jackson, Maria has lived in almost complete seclusion with her family. Cautiously at first, and always unobserved by other villagers, Barnard begins calling on Maria and slowly wins over her affections. Indeed, he even encourages her to leave the cottage on some evenings so that they might be alone together. The spot he picks for these clandestine meetings is the Red Barn.

Now Maginn's story moves swiftly towards its climax. After several months Maria becomes pregnant and, barely able to conceal his anger, Barnard says the child must be got rid of. And shortly after its birth he callously poisons the baby and orders the terrified Maria to help him bury the body. Hardly has this problem been resolved, than Hannah Woods reappears and begs Barnard to help her secure the release of 'Beauty' Smith from Newgate where he has been imprisoned for theft. Loath as he is to aid the woman who deceived him, Barnard feels that he owes Smith some help - all the more so because of the thefts he himself was involved in and which only Smith's silence can prevent him from being implicated in. Because Barnard is far from being a wealthy man - having drained much of his inheritance by his earlier wild living - Hannah suggests he should advertise for a wife and try and attract an heiress. If he won't help, she warns, she will expose all his earlier indiscretions.

Now Barnard is beset on both sides. Maria is pressing him to marry her, threatening to reveal what happened to her child if he does not, while Hannah holds his future in jeopardy with her knowledge of his past. He agonises over the problem and decides he must remove one or other of the women. He fears the cunning Hannah too much for it to be her - and so realises it must be the luckless Maria. In a moment of inspiration he decides to lure her to the Red Barn where they have met so often and there murder her.

In the closing chapters, Maginn parallels the facts of the real case by describing how Barnard/Corder makes an arrangement for Maria to go to the barn disguised as a man, there kills her, and buries the body. He then disappears to London, finds a wealthy bride, and discharges his obligations to 'Beauty' Smith. Just as he fondly imagines his troubles are over, Maria's mother has the first of her dreams about her daughter being murdered, and the chain of events begin which lead inexorably to the arrest and conviction of Barnard.

William Maginn adds just one imaginative piece of fictionalisation to the end of his story with the reappearance of Stafford Jackson, determined once again to prey on Barnard. However, when he learns of the young landowner's disappearance coincidental with that of Maria, he begins to suspect that Barnard may well have murdered the girl. He is in fact busy disclosing these facts to Maria's father just after Mrs. Marten has had the third of her dreams, and together they convince old Marten to go and look in the Red Barn. After the discovery, Jackson is apparently so filled with remorse at having set the girl on the road to ruin that he recklessly tries to rob a stage coach - and is shot and killed by one of the passengers: a handsome young captain who is returning to Polstead after years abroad in the hope of winning the hand of the girl he has always loved. It is none other than Harry Everton. A nice twist of literary justice!

And so - in the words of William Maginn - "the infamous and wretched perpetrator of the atrocity" is traced to London, arrested, brought back to Suffolk for trial, and afterwards duly executed. He concludes, "Thus perished William Barnard, in the prime of youth. Such was the just and awful vengeance visited by unerring Heaven on the head of a murderer. Such was the consequences of lawless appetite, of vicious society, of unprincipled folly, and blasphemous infidelity."

That, in simplified form, is the story of *The Red Barn* as narrated by Maginn, and those familiar with the various dramatised versions of the story as produced in the theatre during the past 165 years will no doubt see strong similarities. From the very start, playwrights have utilised the elements of Maginn's characterisation of Corder as a heartless landowner steeped in vice and Maria as the cruelly-wronged village maiden, for their own stage versions. Like him they have taken a variety of liberties with the facts of the case, but stuck to the major developments of the tragedy, in particular Maria's pregnancy by Corder, her being lured to the Red Barn in disguise, and the eventual discovery of her body as a result of the uncannily prophetic dream experienced by her stepmother.

Records indicate that the story of the murder became a popular subject for plays immediately the events began to be unfolded. The very first such drama may well have been "The Late Murder of Maria Marten" presented at Polstead Fair in July 1828, *before* Corder had even gone to trial, and there is little doubt that within weeks of his execution the story was being acted in small provincial theatres, on portable stages (or 'fit-ups' as they were known), in fairground booths and even in barns, to the delight of ever-increasing audiences. As H.G.Hibbert tells us in his *Playgoer's Memories*, "Maria's murder was depicted on the stage with all the alert enterprise of the modern cinema." (Incidentally, the term for a successful production as a "Barnstormer" originated from just such presentations!)

It is likely that these earliest dramatisations had only the most rudimentary scripts and the actors ad-libbed and adapted the story to suit themselves and their audiences. Theatre histories indicate that such performances delighted in evocative titles like "The Mysterious Murder", "The Gypsy's Curse" and - especially for London audiences - "Advertisement for Wives". Hibbert also makes another interesting comment on these early productions in his book when he speaks about the only one of Maria Marten's three illegitimate children who survived - Thomas Henry, her son by Peter Mathews.

"This offspring," he writes, "lived many years in Colchester, and would threaten to invoke the magistrates to prevent performances of 'Maria Marten' by players unless he were mollified - surely the most curious collection of royalties ever known!"

The earliest theatre poster for the play still in existence is for a performance in Lincoln in October 1830 when it was called "The Red Barn; or the Prophetic Dream" and I have reprinted this along with another typical example dated ten years later for The Marylebone Theatre, London, when the story was an established favourite with big city audiences as well. Montague Slater in his introduction to *Maria Marten; or The Murder in the Red Barn*, perhaps the best of all the Victorian stage versions of the story, says that "the play is perhaps the most famous of all the melodrama written for the popular theatres". It was probably not until as late as 1842 that a printed version of the play came into existence, and the many adaptions which followed all drew to a degree on each other, as well as Maginn's novel and Curtis's newspaper reports.

H.G.Hibbert informs us that a popular feature in several of these versions was the appearance of Maria as a ghost who told William sitting in the condemned cell, "William, William, thy poor Maria pities - pities and forgives thee." Another version was climaxed by the execution of Corder on the stage! He writes, "An elaborate 'set' of the scaffold and the actual enactment of the execution was reserved for gala nights. There is record of an ugly disturbance when once, at Cambridge, the performance stopped short of this delectable scene. The manager apologised that the actor was suffering from overwork - and even declined to accept the suggestion he should 'take a curtain', duly haltered, by way of a compromise. After a little controversy 'the audience slowly and with manifest reluctance left the house'."

Perhaps, though, the best known version of the story is *Maria Marten* which the last great 'Master of Melodrama' Tod Slaughter (1885-1962) presented at the old Elephant & Castle Theatre in London from 1927

THEATRE, LINCOLN.

BY DESIRE OF

G. E. WELBY, Esq. M.P. & C. FURNOR, Esq.

THE STEWARDS OF THE STUFF BALL.

On *WEDNESDAY Evening,* OCTOBER 27th, 1830,

Will be presented, the celebrated drama of

Sweethearts and Wives.

Admiral Franklin, ... Mr. SHIELD.		Charles Franklin, ... Mr. SIMMS.	
Sandford, ... Mr. CULLENFORD		Curtis, ... Mr. HODGSON.	
Billy Lackaday, ... Mr. GURNER.			
Mrs. Bell, ... Mrs. DANBY.		Susan, ... Mrs. GURNER.	
Eugenia, ... Mrs. W. ROBERTSON.		Laura, ... Miss STEWART SMITH.	

A COMIC SONG ...... by ...... Mr. HODGSON.

With (for the LAST TIME,) the new Tragic Melo Drama, in 4 Acts, founded on Fact, called the

RED BARN;

OR, THE PROPHETIC DREAM.

THE MUSIC SELECTED AND ARRANGED BY MR. STANNARD

WITH NEW SCENERY PAINTED FOR THE OCCASION BY MR. SIMMS.

Mr. ROBERTSON is induced to bring forward this piece, not only from the unprecedented success it has been received with at the various Theatres in the Kingdom, but as a moral lesson, that Murder, however for the time concealed, will speak with most miraculous organ. Every one must be aware of the Incidents on which the Piece is founded, but the Dramatist has avoided the real names of the parties, still blending all the principal Incidents, with an effect at once awful and instructive.

Cordel, a young Farmer, ... Mr. HAMILTON.
Mr. Delamere, a Magistrate, ... Mr. BRUNTON.
Wilton, a Gipsy Confederate of Cordel, ... Mr. TALBOT.
Marlin, a labouring Farmer in the vale of years, ... Mr. STYLES.
Robin, a Factotum to Chatteral, ... Mr. SIMMS.
Peter Christopher Chatteral, a Barber, Beadle, &c. .... Mr. GURNER.
Nell Hatfield, a Gipsy, .. Mrs. W. ROBERTSON. Anna Hatfield, her daughter, .. Mrs. GURNER.
Dame Marlin, ... Mrs. DANBY. Mrs Cordel, ... Mrs. HAMILTON.
Maria Marlin, ... Miss STEWART SMITH.

A Brief Sketch of the Incidents:
CORDEL for his numerous Crimes receives the CURSE of the GIPSY CHIEF.
CORDEL'S FIRST MEETING WITH MARIA MARLIN.
His promise to marry her—The anguish of old Marlin and his Dame at parting with her—His proposition to meet her at the RED BARN disguised in Man's Apparel—Her joy at the thoughts of Marriage.

AWFUL MEETING AT THE RED BARN,

WHERE THE DEED IS PERPETRATED.

THE APPEARANCE OF MARIA TO HER MOTHER IN A DREAM.

The Interior of the Barn where the Body is discovered.

CORDEL's Marriage in London.—His living in splendour when the GIPSY's CURSE is fulfilled.

CORDEL'S APPREHENSION AND CONFESSION,

And the appearance of the Shade of Maria Marlin in Cordel's Dream, which produces the denouement.

Among the minor Incidents to give effect to the serious part of the Melo-drama, some Comic Parts are introduced which must set gravity at defiance.

The playbill for one of the earliest stage productions about the crime, 'The Red Barn; or The Prophetic Dream', first performed in Lincoln in October 1830.

onwards, and then made into an even more successful film in 1935. Slaughter, born Norman Carter Slaughter in Newcastle-on-Tyne, was also known as 'Mr. Murder' and 'The Demon Barber' because of his speciality of playing blood-curdling roles during a career which lasted for half a century. He actually made his debut on stage at the tender age of 14, but it was not until he had grown to maturity, six foot tall with a barrel chest, flickering eyebrows and a sinister, throaty chuckle, that he found his metier playing in Grand Guignol productions.

Although Slaughter made a speciality of murder most foul on the stage, it was said that in his private life he could not even bring himself to kill one of the chickens which he raised in his Surrey home. And despite his popularity as "the most lovable multi-murderer on the stage", he was frequently in financial trouble and in 1953 had a receiving order for bankruptcy issued against him for back taxes. But even this could not entirely dampen the spirits of the veteran actor who appeared in over 500 plays and sketches playing such famous villains as Sweeney Todd, Dr Jekyll, Long John Silver, the grave-robber Hare, Jack the Ripper and, of course, William Corder.

Slaughter's over-the-top acting style - especially when playing Corder as a smarmy, unscrupulous lecher - for years filled the Elephant & Castle Theatre where he was also the actor-manager for a time. He was never sparing in his use of blood and would delight in spraying the front rows of the stalls with great globs of rich-red cochineal which spurted from his property razor! In 1934 he entered the world of films, and the following year made the first screen version of 'Maria Marten' or 'The Murder in the Red Barn', an eighty-minute, black and white epic filmed almost entirely on studio sets, which has since become something of a cult classic - particularly with American college students where the movie is frequently shown on late-night television. A recent synopsis in *TV Times* for a midnight screening of the film on British TV enthused:

"A chance to see the legendary Tod Slaughter in full flow! Eric Portman also made his screen debut in this all-stops-out melodrama about a pregnant maiden in the clutches of a villainous squire."

Those fortunate enough to have seen Slaughter at his eye-rolling, chop-licking best relentlessly pursuing the beautiful and innocent Maria (played by Sophie Stewart), will know how closely he personified the mental picture we now have of the "wicked squire". The stills reprinted in

99

this book will perhaps convince those who have not yet been so fortunate.

By a curious twist of fate, Slaughter died immediately after having given yet another successful Saturday night performance as Corder in 'The Murder in the Red Barn' at the Derby Hippodrome. He was then 70 years old, but as ever his entrances had been greeted by boos and hisses, and his end on the gallows brought cheers that rang the theatre's rafters. This final curtain call was aptly reported by the *Daily Express* in its issue of February 20, 1956:

"He died in his sleep a few hours after being hanged in full view of the audience in 'The Murder in the Red Barn'. No living actor curdled more blood or stormed more barns - for more than 50 years he strangled, throttled and garrotted his way up and down Britain in lurid melodramas. It has been estimated that he killed Maria Marten more than 2,000 times in the Red Barn!"

Even *The Times*, that august newspaper of record, carried a lengthy obituary of the venerable thespian, concluding its notice: "His film of Maria Marten will remind future generations of an actor who was steeped in crime on the stage but was a great favourite in his profession."

Truer words have rarely been written. For the spirit of Tod Slaughter has lived on, not only in re-runs of his film, but in the various new stage versions of the story and adaptations for the radio and television. The number of productions by national theatre companies, repertory companies and amateur dramatic societies is now beyond calculation. Indeed, no other melodrama I am aware of is so popular with actors and audiences everywhere. Ready support for this claim may be found at Samuel French's Theatre Bookshop in London where no less than three different versions of the play are on sale and all feature in the company's annual list of best sellers.

The last decade in particular has seen a number of ingenious stage productions as well as the first television adaptation. In 1978, the Crucible Theatre in Sheffield presented 'Maria Marten' by Peter James, Terry Gilligan and Bill Stewart as their Christmas Show, which mixed social commentary and farce. The following year the Torch Theatre Company addressed the central issue of the legend: Was Maria Marten a rich man's plaything or a heartless tart? The production skilfully put forward both sides of the argument and was well served by Dave Redgrave as Corder and Gabriella Mowbray as Maria. *The Guardian* reviewer thought it "a very ingenious idea" and added, "To show that one of the most popular hangings in history has a strong area of doubt adds a potent argument to the abolitionist case - Corder could hardly have been as black as he was painted or Maria as white."

The mystery of who really was guilty was also utilised by the Hoxton Hill Community Theatre from London's East End in their play 'Who Killed William Corder', staged to mark the 150th anniversary. The production was devised from contemporary accounts and explored the relationships of the characters involved in the murder as well as introducing some that were not commonly associated with it. The second act was memorable for its switching between real events and actions inside Corder's mind.

In December 1980, *BBC Television* presented the first major small screen production of the legend in 'Maria Marten or The Murder in the Red Barn. The three-part drama of hour-long episodes was written by Douglas Livingstone who visited Polstead and formed some strong opinions about the case while writing his script.

"The truth is that Maria was the village whore with three illegitimate children," he said in an interview in *Radio Times* before the screening of the first episode on December 28. "And Corder wasn't such a bad lad. But the Victorians switched the facts to make a moving melodrama. I've tried to redress the balance of sympathies."

Because it was felt by the BBC that Polstead was not suitable for all the location shooting - though a number of key scenes were filmed in the village - the production team also set up their cameras at Great Saxham, Cockfield and Bungay, and were well received by residents in all four places. Douglas Livingstone, though, remembered his first visit to Polstead somewhat ruefully.

"After I'd carefully researched through all the old documents and records I decided to go to the actual scene of the crime," he recalled. "I asked for directions to the Red Barn and was given them. I plodded through mud and mire - and found nothing. When I got back I was told, 'Oh, they pulled it down 100 years ago!'"

Nonetheless, Livingstone's storyline authentically evoked both the period and the story and speculated how the separate dreams of Maria and Corder - he to be a teacher and she a fine lady - drew them fatefully together. Pippa Guard and Kevin McNally played the lead roles, with Trevor Peacock as the evil catalyst in the murder, 'Beauty' Smith. There was a strong local connection in the shape of actor Jon Laurimore, who played the astute constable James Lea, for he has lived in Boxford for many years.

Both public and press were full of praise for the production; Herbert Kretzmer of the *Daily Mail* writing on December 30: "Stringently avoiding the excessive theatricality that has degraded this story for 165 years, Jane Howell's spare, intelligent production placed the story firmly within the class context of its period. Maria was sympathetically seen as a plaything/ victim of the oppressive morality of the time. It was a dark, chill story with hardly a hint of the farmyard freshness and starched gingham of the Hovis commercial."

I am certain that, following the success of this serial, we shall see further versions of the story on both TV and the stage investigating the squalid realities of rural life in the early years of the nineteenth century, as it undoubtedly was for many people in Polstead - and much of East Anglia, for that matter. But I am equally sure that no amount of sociological or psychological explanation will ever dim what is now a legend forever established in the annals of crime.

So, as I said right at the start of this book, the lure of the murder still draws people from the far corners of the earth to Polstead to look at the pretty cottage where Maria lived, at William Corder's house overlooking the village pond, and at the small memorial tablet in the graveyard of St Mary's Church. Many will also, no doubt, search in vain for the most famous of all the localities, the Red Barn, despite the fact that all traces have long since disappeared.

No doubt the interest in this bizarre murder, with its elements of the sordid and the supernatural that has given us the archetypal figures of melodrama, has far from run its course. Maria Marten may well have gone to an ill-deserved fate - though she was not the pure soul legend would have us believe - and William Corder may indeed have been painted in blacker colours and more summarily executed than he deserved; however what remains beyond dispute is that both have found a place in record more enduring than almost any other figures in the entire history of crime. And the reason for that, and what it tells us of human nature, may well be the greatest mystery of all where the story of The Red Barn is concerned.

MARYLEBONE THEATRE,

LICENSED PURSUANT TO ACT OF PARLIAMENT.

On Monday, April 6th, 1840,

The Performance to Commence with a Drama, in **Two Acts**, entitled

THE RED BARN,

William Corder. . Mr. Pennett,   Farmer Martin. . Mr. Robotham,
George, (his Son) Miss Robotham,   Timothy Bobbin. . Mr. J. Douglass,
Johnny Rawbold. . Mr. Mellon,   Mr. Lee. (the Officer) Mr. Robberts,   Mr. Moor...Mr. Curling
Waiter, Mr. Lewis,   John. . Mr. Cave,
Maria. . Mrs. Douglass.   Dame Martin. . Mrs. Robotham,   Sally. . Mrs. Robberts.

SONG.   " *The Charity Girl,*"   by   Master MARS.
NEAPOLITAN HORNPIPE.   -   BY   -   **MISS WHITE.**

The crime at Polstead soon became one of the most popular melodramas and packed theatres throughout the length and breadth of Victorian England.

The 'Wicked Squire' personified - Tod Slaughter played William Corder over 2,000 times on the stage!

*A selection of stills
from*
Tod Slaughter
in
**MARIA
MARTIN**
or
**The Murder
in the Red Barn**
*Courtesy of the National Film
Archive/Stills Library*

A selection of stills
from
Tod Slaughter
in
MARIA
MARTIN
or

The Murder
in the Red Barn
Courtesy of the National Film
Archive/Stills Library

106

ENVOIE

* * *

F OR ALMOST all of the 165 years since the crime occurred there has been argument and discussion as to whether William Corder was actually responsible for the murder of Maria Marten. Numerous theories have been developed around the case, in particular because of the prejudiced manner in which Corder's trial was conducted, and the unsatisfactory evidence of several witnesses. Corder did, of course, initially claim to be innocent of the girl's murder - claiming that she committed suicide - but then retracted this claim shortly before his execution.

One of the stoutest defences for Corder was mounted by Donald McCormick in his investigative book, *The Red Barn Mystery*, in which he resurrected a great deal of contemporary material - much of it hearsay, it has to be said, and to quite a substantial degree based on old gossip from Polstead, which we can see had been prompted by all the imaginative retellings of the story like Maginn's novel, *The Red Barn*. In essence, McCormick's claim is that while Corder certainly did shoot and critically wound Maria in the Red Barn, he panicked after the incident and rushed away to find some implements to bury the girl, unaware that she was not yet dead. While he was away, the nefarious 'Beauty' Smith came across the bleeding and helpless Maria and finished off the job, thereby giving himself a hold over the unknowing Corder.

Another school of thought has cast grave doubts on the authenticity of Anne Marten's claim to have dreamt where the body of her murdered stepdaughter lay. It has been suggested that she knew all along about the murder and finally revealed the whereabouts when certain of her plans were thwarted. This line of reasoning has been advanced by Dorothy Gibbs and Herbert Maltby in their intriguing work *The True Story of Maria Marten* (1949). They believe that Anne Marten (who was, after all, a young woman) may well have been having an affair with William Corder herself. At one juncture they write "Polstead folk maintain that, anxious to get rid of Maria, and conscious of William's tendencies, Mrs. Marten implanted in his mind the idea of killing Maria." The authors believe that Anne Marten wanted William Corder all to herself, and it was only when he disappeared (marrying and settling in London) and failed to keep in touch with her and honour a promise he made to send regular supplies of money, that she "invented" the dream as a means of revenging herself against her former lover.

A third important theory has been developed by Leslie Sheen of Bury St. Edmunds who believes that Maria threatened a mock suicide when she met her lover in the Red Barn. Corder apparently had told her he had changed his mind about marrying her, so, in an attempt to frighten him, she pointed a pistol at herself. Inadvertently she pulled the trigger, the gun went off, and the bullet went through her right eye. At this moment, as Corder stood aghast and unable to decide what to do, 'Beauty' Smith, his partner in crime - who had been hiding unobserved, watching the meeting - emerged from his vantage point. Without compunction, he seized a knife and stabbed the screaming Maria to death. The men then buried the body and Corder hurried off to London. When he was arrested, Mr Sheen maintains, Corder was too frightened of Smith to implicate him in the crime.

"I am convinced that there was a complete miscarriage of justice", says Mr. Sheen. "The Crown and the courts conspired to hang him for a murder he did not commit. So many people only know about the Red Barn incident through a bloodthirsty mystery or sex book. I became interested when I read one of the older books and, like most people, at first felt sympathy for Maria. When I read deeper I began to question some of the assumptions."

Mr. Sheen also thinks that Maria's stepmother was the lover of 'Beauty' Smith, who had introduced Corder and Maria into London criminal circles. Smith, he says, was later deported for stealing a pig and, while in Australia, made a statement that could have cleared Corder. He believes Smith had planned to rob Corder's house and told Maria to arrange for Corder to go to Ipswich to leave the way clear for the burglary. The signs were that he had some kind of hold over Maria.

"But", says Mr. Sheen, "as Smith lay in hiding, Corder and Maria had their row - the row which the Crown prosecutor maintained led to the squire shooting and killing his mistress, and convicted him to death on the gallows."

There are other less convincing theories that have been advanced, but no useful purpose would, I think, be served by expounding them here.

They are all discussed to a fuller degree in the various other books on the murder mentioned in the pages of this volume, and the interested reader is directed to them. My study has no pretentions to present the last word in the case, merely perhaps a more balanced account of the events based on a full examination of the contemporary records.

For my part I remain convinced that William Corder *did* murder Maria Marten in the Red Barn on that afternoon of Friday, May 18, 1927. The only issue I find unresolved and therefore rich with possibilities was whether anyone else was involved, whether knowingly or not. The sinister presence of 'Beauty' Smith certainly seems deeply ingrained in the whole mystery and further investigation may throw new light on his role. Nor is Anne Marten to be put totally above suspicion, particularly when one reads her crucial testimony to the murder trial about the events leading up to the murder. Her recall of details is quite staggering and far better than one might have expected from a young, ill-educated country woman. Indeed, much of our knowledge of the crucial developments in the story is based on her testimony.

In hindsight it is possible to see a great many errors committed by the authorities and lawyers in Corder's trial - mistakes that would have held any modern judiciary up to ridicule and stopped the farce long before the unfortunate accused had been dispatched to the gallows. Yet there is nothing we can do for William Corder now, nor poor Maria for that matter. Just, perhaps, be grateful that it was cases such as theirs which helped establish the painstaking and fair system of justice we enjoy today. That both had to pay for it with their lives is no doubt a higher cost than any of us would have asked, and they only have their notoriety to comfort them wherever they may be.

Peyton House,
Boxford, Suffolk.
June 1979.
Revised June 1992

APPENDIX

* * *

Atrocious Murder of a Young Woman in Suffolk

This is the text of the 'catch penny' broadsheet published by James Catnach in April 1828 immediately after Maria Marten's body had been found in the Red Barn. The pamphlet was subtitled *Singular Discovery of the Body from a Dream* and was illustrated by the two engravings of the barn and the suspect, William Corder, which are reprinted here.

THE RED BARN

THE SCENE OF THE MURDER, AND WHERE THE BODY OF
MARIA MARTEN WAS FOUND CONCEALED.

A murder, rivalling in cold-blooded atrocity that of Weare, has been brought to light within a few days at Polstead, in the county of Suffolk. The circumstances which have reached us are as follows:-

Maria Marten, a fine young woman, aged twenty-five, the daughter of a mole catcher in the above village, formed an imprudent connection, two or three years ago, with a young man, named William Corder, the son of an opulent farmer in the neighbourhood, by whom she had a child. He appeared much attached to her, and was a frequent visitor at her father's. On the 19th of May last she left her father's house, stating, in answer to some queries, that she was going to the Red Barn to meet William Corder, who was to be waiting there with a chaise to convey her to Ipswich, where they were to be married. In order to deceive observers - Corder's relations being hostile to the connection - she was to dress in man's attire, which she was to exchange in the barn for her bridal garments. She did not return at the time expected, but being in the habit of leaving home for many days together, no great alarm was

expressed by her parents. When, however, several weeks had elapsed, and no intelligence was received of their daughter, although William Corder was still at home, the parents became anxious in their inquiries. Corder named a place at a distance where he said she was, but that he could not bring her home for fear of displeasing his friends. Her sister, he said, might wear her clothes, as she would not want them. Soon after this, Corder's health being impaired, he, in real or pretended accordance with some advice he had received, resolved on going abroad. Accordingly, he left home in September last, expressing a great anxiety before he left to have the barn well filled. He took with him about £400. Several letters have been received by his mother (a widow) and sister, as well as by the Martens, in which he stated that he was living with Maria in the Isle of Wight. These, however, bear the London post-mark. He regularly desired that all his letters should be burnt, which request was not complied with. Strange surmises lately gained circulation throughout the neighbourhood, and one person stated, as a singular circumstance, that on the evening when Maria Marten disappeared, he had seen Corder enter the Red Barn with a pick-axe. The parents became more and more disturbed and dissatisfied, and these fears were still more strongly agitated by the mother dreaming, on three successive nights last week, that her daughter had been murdered, and buried in the Red Barn. She insisted that the floor of the barn should be upturned. On Saturday, Marten, the father, with his mole-spade and a neighbour with a rake, went to examine the barn, and soon, near the spot where the woman dreamt her daughter lay buried, and only about a foot and a half under ground, the father turned up a piece of a shawl which he knew to have belonged to his daughter, and his assistant with his rake pulled out part of a human body. Horror-struck, the unhappy father and his neighbour staggered from the spot. The remains were afterwards disinterred, the body being in a state of decomposition. The pelisse, shawl, Leghorn bonnet, and shoes, were, however, distinctly identified as those once belonging to Maria Marten. The body has been closely inspected but, owing to its decayed state, no marks of violence have, we understand, been discovered, except some perforations in the bones of the face, which appear as if made by small shot. There can be but little doubt left but that this unfortunate young woman fell a victim to her unhallowed passion, and was inhumanly butchered by the monster upon whom she relied for future protection as a husband. The barn is well situated for such a deed of horror, being a full quarter of a mile from any human habitation. An inquest was held before W. Weyman, Esq., Coroner for the Liberty, on Sunday last, and adjourned till Friday, in the hope that some intelligence may be gained of Corder to lead to his apprehension. The murdered remains were buried on Sunday night, at Polstead, in the presence of an immense concourse of spectators.

Printed by J. Catnach, 2, Monmouth Court, 7 Dials.

* * *

William Corder's advertisement which appeared in the 'Sunday Times' of November 25, 1827 and which resulted in around one hundred replies.

" *Matrimony.*—A private gentleman, aged 24, intirely independent, whose disposition is not to be exceeded, has lately lost the chief of his family by the hand of Providence, which has occasioned discord amongst the remainder, under circumstances most disagreeable to relate. To any female of respectability, who would study for domestic comforts, and willing to confide her future happiness to one in every way qualified to render the marriage state desirable, as the advertiser is in affluence. Many very happy marriages have taken place through means similar to this now resorted to, and it is hoped no one will answer this through impertinent curiosity ; but, should this meet the eye of any agreeable lady who feels desirous of meeting with a sociable, tender, kind, and sympathising companion, they will find this advertisement worthy of notice. Honour and secrecy may be relied on. As some little security against idle applications, it is requisite that letters may be addressed (post-paid) A. Z., care of Mr. Foster, stationer, 68, Leadenhall-street, with real name and address, which will meet with most respectful attention.''

116

Advertisement for Wives

A selection of the letters received by William Corder in reply to his advertisement seeking a wife in November 1827. They were collected and published in a small booklet by the London Stationer, Foster, in 1828.

LETTERS SENT BY VARIOUS LADIES
IN ANSWER TO CORDER'S MATRIMONIAL
ADVERTISEMENT
(A Selection)

Nov. 26th, 1827

Sir,

The perusal of your advertisement in the Sunday Times awakened a feeling of sympathy, as I also have been the subject of the chastening hand of Providence.

I do not reply for myself, but having the pleasure of knowing a young and amiable female, in her twenty-third year, and who is highly-accomplished, it occurred to me, that she might prove a companion suited to ameliorate your present sorrows, and enliven your future prospects. You request real names and address; forgive me, Sir, if under the existing circumstances I withhold both, as I think it would be an infringement of the female delicacy, to avow them in the present stage of our correspondence. If you will favour me with an interview on Waterloo Bridge, *between* the hours of *three* and *four* on the afternoon of Wednesday next, I shall be able to communicate every particular to you: that you recognize me, it is necessary to say, that I shall wear a black silk dress, red shawl, and grey muff, claret-coloured bonnet, and black veil; our conversation *must* commence by your presenting me with this note. Believe me when I add, that I am perfectly serious, and have no other motive in addressing you than promoting the happiness of two young persons.

I am, Sir,
Yours very obediently

Monday Evening,
8 o'clock.

Dec. 1st, 1827.

Sir,

In perusing the Times Paper of Nov. 25th, I observed your advertisement for a partner in the marriage life, where you say any *female of respectability*, who would study for domestic comforts, and willing to confide in you, led me to suppose that fortune was not your object, which induced me to make the application, though I must say *prudence* whispers it is contrary to the rules of decorum, and I believe this is the first time I have ever deviated from her precepts. I am a female of respectability, my father has been a very *respectable* tradesman, and a man of good fortune, but Providence has now placed me in a more *humble situation*; I have had a good plain education, but no accomplishments. If I have been too presumptuous in addressing one who styles himself an independent gentleman and a man of honour, I trust *this will be buried in oblivion*; but should it be thought worthy of an answer, it much oblige.

Your humble Servant.

P.S. Probably you might like a description of the writer of these lines; - she is of rather short stature, slight made, not handsome, dark complexion, dark hair and eyes, and one who has not wrote out of *impertinent* curiosity, but for particular reasons dare not sign her name in this; but if she have occasion to write a second, you may rely upon it being signed, should this be answered.

Direct for - , Post Office.   To be left till called for.

*

Sir,

Having seen your advertisement in the Sunday Times Newspaper, I beg leave to reply to it; not from any impertinent curiosity, but from a wish that what I state may meet with your approbation. I am the daughter of a respectable tradesman; he is the only one of the family in business. I have a step-mother, and there is a second family, therefore, to prevent any disagreement amongst us, I have left my father's house, and am at this time earning my own living in one of the first establishments in - (not as a milliner or dress maker). My friends are kind enough to say that I possess a good temper, lively disposition, and as to appearance passable, not any pretension to beauty; with regard to property, all I ever expect to be mistress of will be a small income, left me by my mother; it is sufficient to keep me independent when I shall have the misfortune to lose my father, which I hope may be many years ere that event happens. My age is the same as your own, twenty-four, your being in affluent circumstances would not induce me to become your wife, unless I found your disposition and mine could agree, and that in every sense of the word I could love, honour, and obey, with pleasure and gratitude. I think I have said all that prudence will allow. I must add, I think it rather unfair for you to expect a respectable female would like to give her real name and address in the first letter she writes; for although your advertisement reads very fair, there may be *some little trick on your side*; but I am in earnest, and you may depend upon the greatest secrecy. Should what I have said meet your approbation, direct to me, post paid.

Monday Evening, Nov. 26th, 1827.

*

Sir,

On taking up the Newspaper of yesterday, and seeing the word *Matrimony*, induced me carefully to peruse the advertisement; and from the vary affable and condescending manner in which you expressed yourself, appears to convince me that you mean to act honourable, and which has induced me to possess myself of sufficient courage, which requires a female to have to address a gentleman on so delicate and important a subject. My personal attractions I shall leave you to decide upon; my age is twenty-four, and I hope I am endowed with all those endearing qualities which is so essential to render a married life happy, assuring you that a private interview with you is most anxiously wished for; and the place I purpose meeting you tomorrow at twelve o'clock - I shall be walking towards - , distinguished by wearing a black gown, with a scarlet shawl, and black bonnet, white handkerchief in my hand. If not convenient tomorrow, will be there the same hour Wednesday.

I remain,
Your most obedient Servant.

Sir,

In answer to an advertisement in the Sunday Times, expressing your desire of being introduced to a female of domestic habits, and a disposition to ensure happiness in the marriage state, I beg leave to state, I am of a retired and domestic character, having been always under the care of an amiable and prudent mother; I have a tolerable person, perhaps some beauty, nineteen years of age, good tempered, and of an affectionate disposition. I have resided in London about three years; my family is very respectable, but owing to some change in circumstances, my circle of acquaintance is very limited, therefore I have but little chance of forming an establishment; this had induced me to enter into a detail of my own qualifications, - a thing which is repugnant to my feelings.

I feel rather averse to giving my address upon a first communication, if you answer this application, and are serious in the professions you make, I shall not withhold it.

I remain, Sir
Your obedient humble Servant,

*

November 25th, 1827.

When a female breaks through the rules of etiquette, justly pre-scribed for her sex, as a boundary which she must not pass without sacrificing some portion of that delicacy which ought to be her chief characteristic, it must be for some very urgent reason, such as *romantic* love, or a circumstance like the present; and in answering your advertise-ment, I feel that I am in some degree transgressing the law alluded to, and yet the novelty and sentiments of the advertisement itself, so entirely different from the language generally made use of (and which alone induced me to answer it), almost assure me that no improper advantage will be taken of the confidence I place in the honour of the writer; however, as you request that no person will write from motives of curiosity, I trust that no feeling of that nature actuated you in giving me this opportunity; - but enough of preface.

I need not describe my person, as, should an interview take place, you can judge for yourself; and for mental accomplishments, I am as much indebted to nature and good society, as to education; but from my retired habits and present sphere of life, I flatter myself I should be as well calculated to make a domestic man happy, and to enjoy the social charms of domestic life, as if I had received the first *boarding school* education, and mixed largely in the world of fashion. My prospects in life were once brilliant, but when misfortune with her gloomy train of attendants surrounded my family, the scene changed; but I have still some expectations, although, from the tenor of your advertisement, I presume fortune is but a secondary consideration; a companion only is wanted who would sympathize in all your joys or griefs; one who would return kindness with kindness, love for love; and as I perfectly know my own heart as far as regards those qualities, I do not flatter myself when I say that such a companion would I prove, and where confidence was shown, the fullest would be returned; pardon the warmth of my expressions, nor think me forward in offering them, as I am no giddy girl, nor am I a romantic *old maid*, but a warm hearted, affectionate girl, whose age qualifies her to pass between the two characters, being just turned twenty-one. Excuse my saying more on so delicate a subject; my family are of the highest respectability. References of course will be given and required. Waiting your answer,

I remain, Sir,
Yours, very sincerely and respectfully.

*

Sir,

As I was perusing yesterday's Times, I inadvertently cast my eye on your advertisement, which I am induced to answer, not from a motive of curiosity, but for this reason, - that from the general tenor of its contents, it so much resembles my own fate, that I cannot help thinking that our dispositions would in some measure be congenial to each other, and I am very sure that time must glide on much more agreeably when passed in the society of a tender and affectionate companion. To convince you that I am of a respectable family, I will give you a few particulars, which I hope and trust will be kept secret. My father was a - ; I was left an orphan under the guardianship of - , who placed me at a school to be educated for a governess, consequently, I have moved in society perhaps not inferior to the rank you hold, but by a deviation from rectitude, which was occasioned by the too easily listening to the flattery of one whose vows I foolishly believed to be true, I am entirely deserted by my family, and banished from society; nevertheless, I flatter myself that I do not altogether merit such a fate, for I do assure you, that no one could have acted more prudently than I have done since the unfortunate circumstance happened, which has very much destroyed my peace of mind, but I still hope to see better days: I am two-and-twenty years of age, but have not the least pretension to beauty - quite the contrary. I have a sweet little girl, who is my greatest comfort; she is sixteen months old, and is beginning to prattle very prettily. I have no fortune whatever, but am supporting myself by needle-work at present, until I can meet with something more to my advantage. I mention these facts, that you may not be led into any error, for I should be extremely sorry to act with any duplicity towards any one, and I leave you to consider how far your generosity will extend to appreciate my wrongs, and excuse my past misconduct. I trust that upon acquaintance you would find that I possess qualities which may in some measure over-balance, or at least mitigate, those errors which were committed through an affection which I supposed to be mutual, and at the same time honourable, but, alas! have found it quite the reverse. I can only add, that should you wish an interview, I am ready at any time to see you, either at my own abode, which you will find very respectable, or at any place you may appoint, appropriate with the circumstance; and should I prove finally the female of your choice, you may rest assured that nothing should be wanted on my part towards the augmentation of your happiness, and to render your house comfortable.

I am, Sir,

Your humble Servant.

Mrs. -

*

Sir,

In reply to your advertisement in the Sunday Times, Nov. 25th instant, I must confess, on perusing, I felt rather interested on your behalf; at the same time I am surprised a gentleman possessing so many good qualities, in addition to youth and fortune, should be under the necessity of adopting a mode so public; but there is some apology to be made after the reason you give. I am a young person without parents, possessing a small income; would of course have no objection to form an alliance with a gentleman of respectability, gifted with those desirable qualifications. With respect to myself, I have been well educated in the usual mode of polite education, music, &c, and seen a great deal of domestic life, that I flatter myself, having arrived at the age of twenty-five years, I am competent to fulfil the duties of a married life. I say nothing of my personal appearance, as I propose ocular demonstration. You must excuse my giving my real name and address, as I feel rather reluctant, at the first, to comply with your request. If you wish for an interview, you may direct to - .

I am, Sir,
Yours Respectfully,

*

Nov. 26th, 1827.

Sir,
    Your advertisement, which appeared in the Sunday Times, I feel inclined to answer. If you really are inclined to marry, and all is true which you state, I think I am the person: my age is twenty-two, and am happy to say possess a most amiable disposition, can play the piano-forte, and sing tolerably well; also other accomplishments, which I think not worthy of statement. I have always been brought up domesticated, and am quite able to manage, let my situation be what it may; my wish is to settle in life, provided I meet with one who I think deserves such a wife as I shall make. If your intentions are honourable, you will not blame me for requesting your name and address. First, I am sure, if you do want a wife, that you will not lose a good one because she does not give it. If you send me yours, and a few more particulars, then I shall know how better to proceed. I am a young lady, now living in the town of - with my mother, and in a most respectable manner, are known and respected by all in it; therefore must say I should not like to expose myself and family to ridicule: should your advertisement be only for a joke, consequently it would, therefore I must request you to direct to - . Write by return of post if possible, I shall send my servant for the letter, therefore pay the post if you please.
    P.S. I have no fortune until the death of my mother.

Sir,

I beg to answer your advertisement of last Sunday, but *really think it nothing but a frolic*; I know a charming young woman of *no property*, her friends *highly respectable*, nineteen years of age, exceedingly agreeable person, has had the charge of her parents' house these three years, and brought up by a truly amiable and virtuous mother. I can with great truth say, the young lady is not aware of my answering your advertisement. If you think proper, you may address a line to Mrs. - . I hope you will act honourably with regard to the name, as the writer is a married woman. A friend will put this in the twopenny post.

Your obedient Servant.

The young lady has never been attached to any one, nor has she ever left her friends.

*

November 26, 1827.

If the gentleman who inserted an advertisement in the Sunday Times, heading Matrimony, will call at - , and ask to see Miss - , between the hours of twelve and three, to-day, he may have an interview, when every other particular will be most candidly stated; should the advertiser look for accomplishments or beauty, an interview will be unnecessary.

*

Sir,

In reply to your advertisement in the Sunday Times, I take the liberty of informing you I am of a respectable family; my papa having seen a reverse of fortune has occasioned my mamma to enter into a boarding house at - , which, if it meets your approbation, will thank you to call to-morrow evening, between four and five o'clock, as it will be the most likely time of seeing me. This being unknown to my parents, you had better come as if for boarding. I have a sister at home with me, who is twenty-one - my age is twenty-two. I must beg to excuse this bad writing, as it is done in fear.

* * *

The Mystery of Corder's Skull

(A bizarre true mystery recounted by the famous ghost hunter, R. Thurston Hopkins, of the strange phenomena that beset those who owned the murderer's skull.)

The story of Corder's Skull is a record of fact without any embellishment. My father, who was one of the principal actors in it, usually told this tale after supper on Christmas night, and he certainly believed that he was chronicling facts for, at least, he was endlessly tolerant of all the beliefs and vagaries that spring from man's instinctive pursuit of the Unseen. Of sceptical people who were hopelessly insensible to the lure and mystery of the world intangible, he was always very suspicious, and he often found excuses to avoid doing business with them. He spoke of ghosts as though their existence had always been accepted by all sensible people. There seemed no room in him for doubt, for astonishment, even.

But to return to the haunted skull of Corder, the murderer, with which these records open. No story could have been offered with a greater appearance of verisimilitude - there are dates, names, attested statements from eye-witnesses; places and events are openly and correctly stated. The chief percipient, Doctor Kilner, had a well-balanced scientific mind and was entirely free from superstitious fears. It is interesting to note that the doctor's family had been linked up with the relics of the Red Barn Murder for many years. A former surgeon at Bury Jail had tanned the skin and pickled the scalp of Corder, and bequeathed these gruesome relics to Doctor Kilner in his will. In the show cases of Bury Museum (Moyse's Hall) the curious may still examine these exhibits, together with Corder's pistols and the long dagger which pierced the apex of Maria Marten's heart.

But let me tell the story straightforwardly.

The Red Barn Murder is too well known to need any description here. It is sufficient to say that William Corder was hanged in the jail at Bury St. Edmunds for the murder of Maria Marten in the Red Barn at Polstead, Suffolk. Corder was suspected through a woman's dreams - this murder had excited great and marked interest in Suffolk. The streets had been full of puppet-shows representing the scene of the crime. A Methodist preacher had held forth to five thousand persons in the neighbourhood of the barn. On the Monday of the execution all the workmen in Bury struck work in order to see the execution. As early as nine o'clock upwards of a thousand persons assembled; before twelve, seven thousand had collected.

Many years later Doctor Kilner, a well known practitioner at Bury, removed Corder's skull from the skeleton and had it polished, mounted and enclosed in a square ebony box. He found a spare anatomical skull and wired it on Corder's skeleton to take the place of the missing cranium. Doctor Kilner, who was one of my father's closest friends, afterwards said that from the first moment he removed Corder's skull he felt very uncomfortable about "something." Some impalpable quality of that skull disturbed him. He was a man who boasted that he had little time for all "this mumbo-jumbo nonsense about ghosts," and he postulated that even if the skeleton had possessed some kind of supernatural quality, it must have had most of the nonsense knocked out of it by doctors and students during the fifty years it had been an inmate of the hospital But the doctor had to admit that all the arrangements connected with the acquisition of the skull had been obstructed and damped by some unpropitious influence. In the first place, the doctor had taken Corder's skull by "stealth," in the middle of the night as he did not care to be interrupted *in flagrante delicto* at such a ghoulish job. Having arrived at the museum of the hospital, he lit three candles. As soon as he had lit them one of them snuffed itself out. He turned to light it, and the flames of the other two candles vanished. All the while he was engaged in securing the skull the candles behaved in this ill-natured way: first one and then the other candle winked at him and then went out. But somehow he kept at least one candle alight while he was working. Doctor Kilner placed the skull in a cabinet in his drawing room, and a few days later a most disturbing thing happened.

After surgery hours - about seven o'clock in the evening - a servant came to the doctor and told him a gentleman had called to see him. The doctor was rather irritated at being disturbed in his leisure hours and asked the servant if the caller was anyone she had seen before. No, the servant had never see the gentleman before and added: "He was proper old-fashioned looking, and wearing a wholly furry top hat and a blue overcoat with silver buttons."

Rather against his will the doctor went to meet the caller who was waiting in the surgery in the twilight, telling the servant to bring in a lamp. The doctor said that when he looked into the room it was rather dark, but

126

there might have been someone waiting by the window. However, he had a sensation perfectly independent of sight and hearing that assured him that he was not alone in the room. The maid followed almost on his heels with the lamp and when the light fell on the room the caller had vanished.

The doctor chaffed the maid and told her she must have been dreaming: but she was quite positive that a gentleman had called. Perhaps he had the toothache and it suddenly "stopped like," and thinking better about having the tooth out he had made off without waiting for the forceps. She remembered that some gentleman had rushed out like that a few months back - "It do take gentlemen like that at times."

A few days passed and the doctor had nearly forgotten about his mysterious visitor and all connected with him. But one evening, looking out of his drawing room window, he saw somebody lurking by a summer house at the end of his lawn, and he could just see that he was wearing a beaver hat and a great coat of antique cut. When he stepped into the garden

William Corder's skeleton photographed in the old West Suffolk General Hospital where it was used until 1949 for teaching anatomy to student nurses.

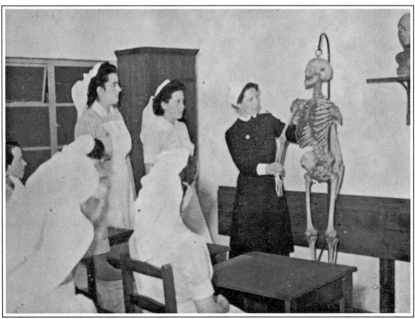

127

the figure vanished. After this a gnawing feeling of uneasiness commenced to invade his thoughts that perhaps he was suffering from the pangs of a guilty conscience for having disturbed the remains of the dead murderer to gratify a personal whim. Anyway, it resulted in a conviction that someone was always dogging his footsteps. He, whoever he was, seemed very anxious to have a heart-to-heart talk with the doctor, but his voice and presence did not seem quite strong enough to accomplish this desire. At night "someone" opened doors, walked about through the house, stood breathing heavily and muttering outside bedroom doors, and, occasionally the members of the household heard a frantic hammering and sobbing below in the drawing room. And all this time, through a maze of dreams, the doctor felt sure that someone was pleading and begging him to listen and attend to his needs.

This was getting tiresome; what with the uneasiness of mind it caused, and the watching and waiting for someone who would not come out in the open and declare himself, the doctor had no sleep for two or three weeks. Of course, the skull in the cabinet downstairs was the cause of all the trouble. There could be but little doubt that the ghost of Corder would go on making things very unpleasant until his skull had been returned. Well, anyway, the idea of returning Corder's skull to the skeleton in the hospital could not be considered. The highly polished tortoise-shell gloss would attract attention. It would be very hard to explain away the sudden change in the appearance of the murderer's cranium. And so he made up his mind to wait a few more days, and then if his ghostly tenant did not settle down and cease his nightly perambulations he would have to think of some way he could get rid of the skull.

The following night the doctor left his bedroom door wide open, just to see what would happen. He tumbled into bed, and immediately fell fast asleep. An hour or two later he awoke suddenly. Some noise had disturbed him. What was it? The sound was on the landing outside - no, not actually on the landing - but downstairs. Should he call out and arouse the household? No, his curiosity was checked by his wish not to appear a panic-monger. He remained in bed, with his knees making a tent of the bed clothes, for some minutes. After watching and waiting, he got cautiously out of bed, lit a candle and walked out on the landing. He held the candle over the stair-rail and below could just see the glass handle of the drawing room door reflecting the light from its many facets. Suddenly, as he looked, the glass knob was blotted out. A hand was on the knob - he could see it quite distinctly. But apparently the hand belonged to no-one. He could not see any figure near it. Yet there it was, a white hand, clearly before his eyes! And then the handle was slowly and softly turned by the phantom hand. He could just hear the faint squeak of the bolt as it turned in the lock-case. There was the door gradually and stealthily opening. No mistake about that. While the doctor was gazing at it with intense wonder he was almost knocked down by a terrific explosion. It had sounded something like the report of a blunderbuss being fired.

The feelings which this explosion stirred in the doctor were a sudden spasm of rage, and a great loathing for the skull he had so foolishly "lifted." He dashed down the stairs, pausing to pick up the heavy plated candlestick as a weapon and rushed to the drawing room. At the doorway he was met with a tremendous gust of wind, and his candle went out. But was it wind? It seemed like a powerful, menacing form which enveloped rather than touched him. He fought his way into the darkness of the room, scratching away at a match. As the match flamed and the room emerged from darkness his attention was caught by a litter of black splinters on the pale Indian carpet. Two or three ideas of what they might be passed through his mind rapidly, but he quickly realised what had happened. The box which had held the skull was broken into a thousand fragments. His gaze travelled to the cabinet which had held the skull resting snugly in its box. The door was open and there on a shelf was the skull grinning malevolently at him.

There is really nothing more to add to this part of the skull's adventures but, as you may imagine, the doctor lost no time in casting the ghostly trophy out of his house. Anyway, from that time the doctor's views on ghosts and the world of spirits were not quite so inclined to the "mumbo-jumbo nonsense" school of thought.

Doctor Kilner insisted upon my father taking Corder's skull as a present, remarking to him:

"As you are the owner of Corder's condemned cell and the gallows on which he was hanged, perhaps it won't hurt you to take care of his skull."

Walking back to Gyves House with the skull in a silk handkerchief my father twisted his foot on one of the steps of the Angel Hotel and fell heavily, just as Lady Gage was passing. The skull rolled maliciously at her feet. My father was fond of telling us about this bizarre encounter. Lady Gage sprang back with a cry of alarm. For a moment her eyes fixed on my father wide-open, questioning and accusing; and then she passed on without saying a word. How could my father explain things to her? As he said afterwards, he felt "drunk and incapable and in charge of a lunatic's skull." What Lady Gage thought about it, my father never found out, for she never referred to the matter afterwards.

As a result of the twisted foot, my father had to remain in bed for a week. The following day his best mare rolled over the side of a chalk pit and broke her back. In the next few months my father knew illness, sorrow and financial disaster. With Doctor Kilner he had embarked on several very successful land and property deals, but suddenly the tide turned and, overtaken by heavy losses, they were both swept to the verge of bankruptcy.

My father decided to break the evil spell of the skull, and took it out to a country churchyard near Bury St. Edmunds and bribed a gravedigger to give the thing a Christian burial. After some weeks of peace and one or two strokes of good fortune, he thanked Heaven that he had cast the evil relic out of his house.

You will say that this story is an invention. But you will be greatly mistaken. Names, places and events are openly and correctly stated, and can be verified. So if ever you come across a tortoiseshell-tinted skull in a japanned cash box, leave it severely alone. If you take it home there will be the Devil to Pay - and you may not be prepared to meet his bill.

* * *

Sunday Times.

No. 303.]   LONDON, SUNDAY, AUGUST 10, 1828.   [Price 7d.

The Trial of William Corder

Extracts from the full report of the trial of William Corder,
held on Thursday and Friday August 7 and 8, 1828,
as appeared in the *Sunday Times* dated August 10, 1828.

*'A correct likeness' of William Corder taken in Bury Jail previous
to his trial for the Murder of Maria Marten in the Red Barn.*

TRIAL OF WILLIAM CORDER.

The extraordinary case of this man having occupied so much of public attention, created a great sensation at Bury St. Edmund's, where the trial was to come on. On Monday last, at 12 o'clock, Chief Baron Alexander took his seat on the bench, for the purpose of proceeding with the criminal business. Long before he entered the court it was crowded to suffocation, by persons anxious to hear the charge, it being understood that allusion would be made to the case of Corder, in the learned Baron's address to the grand juries. We mention juries, for, by a peculiar jurisdiction in this county, two juries are empannelled at each general gaol delivery—one for the liberty and borough of Bury St. Edmund's, and the other for the county at large; to each of which is allotted the investigation of such offences as may have occurred in their peculiar districts. On their being empannelled, the learned Judge addressed them briefly, but took no notice whatever of the case which had brought so many persons together.

The grand juries then retired to their respective jury-rooms, to investigate the several bills that were to be laid before them, and several being sent down as found, business was proceeded on. A true bill for wilful murder against William Corder was returned by the grand jury at 20 minutes to 8 o'clock on that evening.

THURSDAY.

The anxiety to witness the trial of this prisoner was manifested by the assembling of hundreds of well-dressed persons, of both sexes, round the front and back entrances to the Shire Hall, at the early hour of five o'clock in the morning; and notwithstanding the rain continued to fall incessantly, they remained (except those who were carried away in a state of exhaustion from the pressure of the dense crowd) till nine o'clock, when the Lord Chief Baron (Alexander) arrived near the Hall. The external regulations were so bad, that nearly a quarter of an hour elapsed before the few javelin-men who were in front of the court could force a passage to give his lordship and the high sheriff ingress to the court. The moment his lordship gained admission, the scene that presented itself in front of the court beggars all description. The barristers who attend this circuit (and amongst them we observed the counsel for the prosecution) were endeavouring to force their way to the Hall-door, sweating and struggling against the opposing pressure of the crowd, and some of them, at the moment they had almost attained their object, were carried back to the verge of the crowd in an exhausted state. When his lordship had taken his seat on the bench, the names of the jury who had been summoned to try the prisoner were called over; but the crowd was so numerous, and the sheriff's force so ineffective, that it was impossible to make way for them into the court. They were, after the lapse of nearly an hour, brought over the heads of the crowd into the passage leading into the Hall; some with their coats torn, their shoes off, and nearly fainting. We never witnessed any thing like it—the pressure of the crowd at the trial of Thurtell, at Hertford, was not a tithe part equal to what presented itself on this occasion.

OPENING SPEECH.

Mr. Andrews : May it please your Lordship and Gentlemen of the Jury—It becomes my painful duty, as counsel for the crown in this case, to lay before you the facts and circumstances upon which you will have to decide upon the guilt or innocence of the prisoner at the bar. It has always appeared to me to be the duty of counsel placed in my situation not to enlarge upon the facts which they have to give in evidence, or to make an aggravated statement to the jury. To this rule, in a case so serious and important as the present, I shall most strictly adhere. It is, however, necessary and proper that I should shortly lay before you the facts which I am instructed I shall be able to prove to you in evidence, in order to give you a general view of the case, and thereby enable you to judge of the importance, weight, and bearing which attaches to each. The prisoner at the bar, William Corder, is the son of respectable parents, who resided at Polstead, in this county. His father, who is now dead, for some time carried on the business of a farmer, to a consi-. derable extent. After his death, his mother, assisted by an elder brother, since dead, and subsequently by the prisoner, continued the same business. Maria Marten, a young woman of more humble parents, resided in the same parish. She had been for some time known to the prisoner, but it was not until 12 months before the 18th of May, 1827, that they became intimate ; the result of which was the birth of an illegitimate child. The young woman was not confined at her father's house, but was removed to a distance ; and about six weeks before the period in question, she returned home with her infant child. The child, which I believe had been always weakly, died in a fortnight after her return.— It is right that I should here tell you, that Corder had been heard to tell Maria Marten that the parish-officers were thinking of having her taken up because of her bastard child, and that some difference was also known to exist between them with respect to a 5l. note. On one occasion, before the 18th of May, last year, Maria Marten was heard to say to the prisoner, " Well, if I go to gaol, you shall go too." Corder, upon that occasion, told her he should make her his wife.

Upon the Lady being found, suspicion fell upon the prisoner, and an active officer was despatched to London in search of him. He was traced to Ealing-lane, where Lea the officer took him into custody, telling him that he was arrested on a very serious charge, about a young woman named Maria Marten, and he asked him if he knew any thing of such a person? The prisoner said, " No." He again asked him if he had ever known such a person, and he said, " No, never." The officer then said, " I have now asked you twice, and I will ask you for the third and last time. Your name is Corder, and you are the person I am in search of ; Did you ever know a young woman named Maria Marten ?" And his answer again was, " No, never." He was taken into custody, and committed to prison.

In the important inquiry before you, you will look only to the evidence, and discharge your duty with justice to the public, the prisoner, and yourselves. Upon the evidence which I have to lay before you, carefully sifted, as it doubtless will be in the cross-examination, I trust that God will lead you to a right conclusion. If, upon that evidence, you should feel upon your minds the slightest doubt, in God's name give the prisoner the benefit of it, by your verdict of acquittal. But if that evidence should lead you to the painful conclusion, that he has murdered Maria Marten, then you can only discharge your duty by finding him guilty.

WITNESSES FOR THE CROWN.

There followed the statements of prosecution witnesses including Anne and Thomas Marten, Ann and George Marten (Maria's sister and brother), Peter Mathews - whose items of correspondence between himself, Thomas Marten and William Corder were produced and read to the court - James Lea, Francis and Phoebe Stowe (neighbours of the Martens), William Pryke, various tradesmen testifying to Corder's possession of pistols and sword, and John Lawton, surgeon, who at great length and in macabre detail described the wounds and condition of the decomposed body of Maria Marten (of which the following is an example):

I saw some blood on the shift, the stays, the handkerchief round the neck, the lawn handkerchief, and the silk handkerchief, and apparently on the bonnet. I don't recollect any part of a shawl. I took off the garters; they were made of narrow white tape. In taking hold of one of the shoes, the foot came off.

These testimonies occupied five full columns of the 'Sunday Times' report.

Phœbe Stowe examined: Lives at Polstead; knows Corder. Her house may be about 30 rods from the barn. It is the nearest cottage to it. Remembers Corder calling on her one day in May last year. It was about one o'clock. She had known him a good many years. He said "Mrs. Stowe, has not your husband got an old spade he could lend me?" She lent him one. She was unwell, and had lately been confined. He said to witness, "You look bad enough, but I'm in such a hurry, I can't stop to talk to you." She had been confined on the 29th April, and was churched that day month. Corder called before she was churched. Does not remember that he ever borrowed a spade of her before. The spade came back. Does not know who brought it. One day last harvest, in her house, Corder talked with her about a child. Witness asked him where the child was that Maria Marten had by him? He said, "That's dead and buried, and she'll never have any more." Witness said, "She is a young woman, and may have more yet." Prisoner said, "No; Maria Marten will have no more children; she has had her number." Witness said, "Neither you nor I can know that." Prisoner said, "I can; I'll be d—d if she'll have any more." Witness said, "You are married to Maria Marten; why don't you live with her?" Prisoner said, "She's where I can go to her any day or any hour, just when I like." Witness said, "Perhaps you are rather jealous when you are away from her; perhaps you think somebody else is with her." Prisoner said, "No; when I am not with her I'm sure nobody else is."

Cross-examined by Mr. Broderick: I am not a gossip; I am not a talkative woman

William Pryke is farming bailiff to Mrs. Corder. Drove Corder away from Polstead on the 18th of September last. The name of Maria Marten was mentioned. Prisoner said, he had not seen her since May. He spoke very highly of her. Witness assisted Thomas Marten in searching the barn. His testimony confirmed Marten's.

Cross-examined: The prisoner had been very ill before I drove him in September over to Colchester; he said that Maria Marten was a deserving girl, and spoke of her with great affection; I was not examined before the coroner; I was there the whole of the day; an application was made to the coroner to have Corder present while the witnesses were being examined before the jury, and he refused. No magistrate was there.

The Lord Chief Baron: This is very unusual, is it not?

Mr. Broderick: Very, my Lord; and it is very improper too for a coroner to act afterwards as an attorney for the prosecution.

Witness continued: The prisoner was a good-hearted man. There have been preachings near the barn, but not in the barn.

Lord Chief Baron: What! preaching? Is not that very unusual?

Mr. Broderick: Yes, my Lord; there were preachings, and thousands of persons present; and the prisoner treated as a guilty man before his trial.

Witness: There were 5,000 persons to hear the parson preach; his name is Young.

Lord Chief Baron: Scandalous! Was the preacher a member of the Church of England?

Witness: No, my Lord, a Dissenter; I know that bills have been placarded about the murder; and also puppet-shows carried about representing the scene of the murder.

Cross-examined: I was bound over to prosecute; I was churchwarden of Polstead; I knew of shows and preachings, but I did not interfere, as I did not know that I had power to interfere; there have been shows in Bury during the assizes on the subject of the murder—a "Camera Obscura;" I did not interfere.

The Lord Chief Baron here, with consent of the counsel, adjourned the proceedings till Friday.

The prisoner, who had during the early part of the day maintained an air of indifference to his awful situation, there being generally a smile playing upon his features, although his eye had a heavy fixedness, occasionally convulsed with a sudden movement, betraying, with a character not to be mistaken, the emotion under which he laboured during the delivery of particular passages in the evidence, seemed to have lost a considerable part of his confidence towards the close of the day. Much of this alteration may, perhaps, be attributable to the fatigue incident to his situation. The fact of the alteration was, however, too apparent to escape observation. His attention was intensely directed towards the surgeon during the whole of his examination. The adjournment took place at half-past six in the evening.

Corder was carried to court between the governor of the prison and a single attendant, in a sort of tax-cart, out of which the prisoner jumped with alacrity. There were some hisses from the crowd, but he was in a moment removed from their presence.

FRIDAY.

The arrangements of this morning, for the admission of the public, were very well managed, and the active interposition of the governor of the prison (Mr. Orridge) had the best effect in keeping the officers of the High Sheriff in their proper places, and preserving the avenues of the court from the pressure of that vast assemblage which yesterday poured in when the doors were opened, with a force so tremendous as to risk the limbs of those who were not sufficiently athletic for active personal resistance. We understand that the Lord Chief Baron, who was himself carried off his legs in endeavouring to pass from his carriage to the door of the Shire Hall, has disavowed having given any such directions as were imputed to him yesterday, and which necessarily led to a scene of confusion and uproar exceeding any thing hitherto observed in trials of this nature. At all events, every reasonable accommodation was this day afforded the public; and the consequence was, a befitting regularity in conducting the proceedings of the court, and the presence of a number of ladies, whose curiosity (yesterday disappointed) was this day gratified by hearing the close of the trial.

At a quarter before nine o'clock, Corder was put to the bar. He was dressed the same as yesterday. On inquiry, it is understood his age is not 40, but about 30 or 32. He rose early in the prison, and was, during the whole of the morning before he was brought to court, engaged in introducing some alterations into his written defence, which were suggested to him late last night by his counsel. His manner was collected, his complexion fresh, and he looked around him at times with seeming cheerfulness. He was not, however, so entirely at his ease as he appeared to be early on the previous day; his head was not so erect,

135

and he repeatedly heaved deep sighs. Immediately on being put to the bar, he put on his spectacles, folded his arms, and displayed an oscillating and swinging motion of his body, while he leaned his back against the pillar of the dock. He hung down his head frequently during the examination of the witnesses.

During the re-examination of Mr. Lawton, the surgeon, this morning, who produced the skull of the deceased, which was handed from the counsel to the jury, and exhibited so as to be observable in its fractured condition to the whole court, the prisoner, who had just taken off his spectacles, replaced them, and beheld attentively this painful spectacle—he inclined his body forward so as to command a full view of the skull ; but as if the effort to sustain his attitude, and evince this expression, had become too great for his nerves, he suddenly flung his back against the pillar, hastily drew off his spectacles, and evidently laboured under the strongest emotion. In a few minutes, however, he rallied, replaced his glasses, took out his pocket-book, and quickly wrote a memorandum to his leading counsel Mr. Broderick, who at once wrote a reply, which the prisoner read with close attention, and on a movement from the learned counsel tore it into the smallest fragments. His solicitor, at the same time, went to the front of the dock, and had a long consultation with him.

At nine o'clock precisely, the Lord Chief Baron took his seat.

A second surgeon, John Charles Nairn, was cross-examined regarding the condition of the body and clothes found in the Red Barn. Other witnesses from the previous day were re-called to corroborate the known physical markings and clothes of Maria Marten.

PRISONER'S DEFENCE.

The prisoner, being called on for his defence, advanced to the front of the bar, took out some papers, and read nearly as follows with a very tremulous voice :—

" I am informed that by the law of England, the counsel for a prisoner is not allowed to address the jury, though the counsel for the crown is allowed that privilege. While I deplore, as much as any human being can, the fatal event which has caused this inquiry, let me entreat you to dismiss from your minds the publications of the public press from the time of its first promulgation to this hour ; let me entreat you, let me dissuade you, if I can, from being influenced by the horrid and disgusting details which have for months issued from the public press—a powerful engine for fixing the opinions of large classes of the community, but which is too often, I fear, though unintentionally, the cause of affixing slander upon innocence. I have been described as a monster, who, while I meditated becoming the husband of this girl to whom I was evincing an affectionate attachment, was actually premeditating and plotting the perpetration of this horrid crime. With such misrepresentations it was natural, perhaps, to expect that an unfavourable impression should have been created against me, and the more so when the accusation went beyond the present case, and was connected with other crimes well calculated to excite prejudice against me. It is natural you should come to this trial with feelings of prejudice ; but as you expect peace and serenity of mind at home, I implore you to banish from your minds all the horrible accusations which have been promulgated, and give your verdict on the evidence alone. Consider, gentlemen, that the attorney for the prosecution is also the coroner before whom the inquest was taken ; and his conduct, in refusing my being present at the inquest, is conduct which you cannot approve. Since my committal, the coroner

136

has been again at Polstead—has got up additional evidence. My solicitor pressed for a copy of the depositions, which were refused. In consequence of these unjust proceedings, I never heard one of the witnesses examined, and cannot therefore have come prepared as I ought to be. The coroner, thus acting in his double capacity, was likely enough, when meditating to act as attorney for the prosecution, to have entertained impressions inconsistent for the fit discharge of his inquisitorial inquiry : and again, as attorney for the prosecution, he was liable to be diverted from the fulfilment of his duties as coroner ; so that I was in this respect, on the threshold of inquiry, exposed to disadvantages from which I ought to have been saved. This, however, was not all : my solicitor remonstrated ; he was not only refused copies of the depositions, but the attorney for the prosecution, without any notice to me, has visited Polstead, and taken examinations upon oath of the different witnesses, and come to this trial prepared with evidence taken behind my back, and pruned down to suit the exaggerations of this case. I therefore am brought to be tried for my life without any fair knowledge of the evidence against me. In consequence of this unjust proceeding on the part of the coroner, how can I controvert, as I might have done were I allowed to hear the witnesses, equivocal facts and highly-coloured statements, of which I am for the first time informed when brought to trial for my life ? Were witnesses to be privately examined, and their evidence clandestinely obtained ? It has been well observed that " truth is strange," sometimes " stranger than fiction." Never was this assertion better exemplified than in this hapless instance. In a few short months I have been deprived of all my brothers, and my father recently before that period. I have heard the evidence, and am free to say, that, unexplained, it may cause great suspicion ; but you will allow me to explain it. Proceeding, my lord and gentlemen, to the real facts of this case, I admit that there is evidence calculated to excite suspicion,—but these facts are capable of explanation ; and convinced as I am of my entire innocence, I have to entreat you to listen to my true and simple detail of the real facts of the death of this unfortunate woman. I was myself so stupified and overwhelmed with the strange and disastrous circumstance, and on that account so unhappily driven to the necessity of immediate decision, that I acted with fear instead of judgment, and I did that which any innocent man might have done under such unhappy circumstances. I concealed the appalling occurrence, and was, as is the misfortune of such errors, subsequently driven to sustain the first falsehoods by others, and to persevere in a system of delusion which furnished the facts concealed for a long time. At first I gave a false account of the death of the unfortunate Maria. I am now resolved to disclose the truth, regardless of the consequences. To conceal her pregnancy from my mother, I took lodgings at Sudbury : she was delivered of a female child, which died in a fortnight in the arms of Mrs. Marten, although the newspapers have so perverted the fact ; and it was agreed between Mrs. Marten, Maria, and me, that the child should be buried in the fields. There was a pair of small pistols in the bedroom ; Maria knew they were there. I had often showed them to her. Maria took them away from me. I had some reason to suspect she had some correspondence with a gentleman, by whom she had a child, in London. Though her conduct was not free from blemish, I at length yielded to her entreaties and agreed to marry her ; and it was arranged we should go to Ipswich and procure a licence and marry. Whether I said there was a warrant out against her I know not. It has been proved that we had many words, and she was crying when she left the house.

I always treated her with kindness, and had intended to marry her. What motive, then, can be suggested for my taking her life? I could have easily gotten over the promise of marriage. Is it possible I could have intended her destruction in this manner? We went, in the middle of the day, to a place surrounded by cottages. Would this have been the case had I intended to have murdered her? Should I have myself furnished the strongest evidence that has been adduced against me? I might, were I a guilty man, have suppressed the time and place of her death; but my plain and unconcealed actions, because they were guiltless, supplied both. Had I intended to perpetrate so dreadful a crime, would I have kept about me some of the articles which were known to be Maria's? Had I sought her life, could I have acted in such a manner? Had I, I would have chosen another time and place. Look at my conduct since. Did I run away? No! I lived, months and months, with my mother. I left Polstead in consequence of my family afflictions. I went to the Isle of Wight. It is said that the passport was obtained to enable me to leave England at any time. No, it was to enable me to visit some friends of my wife's in Paris. Should I have kept her property, had I any thing to fear from their detection. In December last I advertised in the *Times* newspaper the sale of my house, and gave my name and address at full length. Did this look like concealment? You will consider any man innocent till his guilt is fully proved. It now rests with you to restore me to society, or to doom me to an ignominious death. To the former I feel I am entitled—against the latter I appeal to your justice and humanity. I have nothing more to add, but that I leave my life in your hands, aware that you will give me the humane benefit of the law in cases of doubt, and that your Lordship will take a compassionate view of the melancholy situation in which my misfortunes have placed me."

The above was the substance of the prisoner's address. It was delivered, in many parts, in a feeble and tremulous tone of voice, and under considerable emotion. It is clear, from the pronunciation of particular words, that the prisoner is not a man of much education. He trembled a good deal, but not more than a nervous man would manifest in a moment of excitement. He read the address from a copy-book, and, whether from the composition not being his own, or his being near-sighted, he stammered over several words, and infringed the order of the sentences. He was heard with the utmost silence and attention by the court and the jury, and he occasionally drew his eyes from the book and fixed them on the jury-box, as if to ascertain the impression he had made. Towards the close of his address his voice faltered, so as in particular passages to be nearly inaudible. His address, which was delivered between 11 and 12 o'clock, occupied the court about 25 minutes.

WITNESSES FOR THE DEFENCE.

This section occupied merely three short paragraphs of the report, and consisted of statements by Corder's ex-landlord, Wm. Goodwin, and his wife, of Sudbury, and Thomas Hardy, an ex-employee of the prisoner.

Other witnesses gave similar testimony, spoke to his general humane character, but stated no fact of interest.

JUDGE'S CHARGE.

At 20 minutes to 12 the Lord Chief Baron began to sum up the case. He informed the jury that the prisoner at the bar was indicted for the murder of Maria Marten, and that the law required that the mode in which she had come to her death should be particularly stated in the indictment. Before he entered upon the details of the case, he felt it to be his duty to advert to something which had been said by the prisoner as to the prejudices which had been raised against him both in this county and throughout the country generally. It was unfortunate, extremely unfortunate, whenever such prejudices were raised ; for they placed the life of the prisoner more in jeopardy than the ordinary circumstances of the case against him. Sorry, indeed, was he to say, that, as society was constituted at present, they could not be avoided. Accounts of this transaction, it appeared, had also found their way into the newspapers. Those accounts only related to the charge at the commencement of the business—they contained an *ex-parte* statement of it, without giving the prisoner an opportunity of urging any thing in his defence against it ; and that was certainly a mischief, and an injury to him. The jury, however, had a more impartial task to perform ; they had to decide this issue by hearing the evidence on both sides, whereas hitherto the public had heard one side only.

They had heard it that day asserted, that this poor woman had committed suicide ; but even according to the story which they had heard, it was very strange that immediately on being left alone she should use such various instruments to destroy herself ; for it appeared, in the first place, that she must have fired a pistol at herself, and then, either before or after firing it, have given herself sundry stabs in very different parts of her body,

What had struck him from the beginning of the defence to the end as the most extraordinary feature in it was, the manner in which this alleged suicide was committed. It often happened that these poor girls, when disappointed in their expectations, did lay in hands on themselves ; but then the mode of their death was in general very simple. In this case, if they were to credit the evidence of the surgeons, the wounds inflicted on the body of Maria Marten were of a double description. There were, first, the wounds in the eye, and in the cheek, inflicted by a ball, and then the wounds inflicted with a sharp instrument, that was broader on one side than the other, on the heart and ribs, and the wound inflicted with a similar instrument on the vertebræ of the neck behind the skull. It was extraordinary that instead of hanging herself upon a tree, as poor girls usually did in such circumstances, she should have used two different means to kill herself—the one by shooting herself with a pistol, which was a very unusual weapon for a woman to kill herself with—and the other by stabbing herself with a sharp instrument. The jury must decide on the credibility of the medical witnesses, who ventured to speak as to these two distinct causes of Maria Marten's death, independently of the third mode of death by strangulation, to which one of them had spoken ; and then, if they decided that the wounds had been inflicted in the manner in which the surgeons described, they must decide how far it was possible such multifarious wounds were inflicted by herself. These were the facts of the case as proved in evidence ; and he trusted in God that they would lead them to a proper decision upon it. If they had any doubt upon it, they would give the prisoner the benefit of it ; but if they were satisfied that his representations were false, and that the crime of murder on Maria Marten had been committed by him, then it would be their duty, serving their country manfully and discharging faithfully the solemn oath which they had sworn, to bring in a verdict of guilty against the prisoner, regardless of the consequences by which it might be followed.

The Foreman of the Jury then addressed the Court on behalf of his fellow-jurors, and said that they wished to retire, as the case required some time to be spent in deliberation upon it.

The Lord Chief Baron immediately ordered a bailiff to be sworn to attend them, and at 25 minutes to two the jury retired.

At ten minutes past two, they came back into court, and their Foreman returned a verdict of Guilty against the prisoner.

At this moment, and in the short interval which elapsed between the declaration of the verdict and the declaration of the sentence of the Court, a slight confusion arose before the bar where the prisoner was standing, relative to the possession of the pistols, by which the murder was committed. Lea, the officer, claimed them as his property, in consequence of a promise which he had received from the prisoner when he first apprehended him; Mr. Orridge claimed them as the property of the Sheriff, in consequence of the verdict which had just been recorded against the prisoner. Mr. Orridge remained in possession of them, as the contest was stopped by the crier's proclaiming silence, as the Lord Chief Baron was going to pass sentence on the prisoner.

The prisoner was then asked in the usual form, whether he had any thing to say why he should not die according to law. On his saying nothing,

The Lord Chief Baron addressed him in the following terms:—" William Corder, it is now my painful duty to announce to you the near approach of the close of your mortal career. You have been accused of murder, which is almost the highest offence that can be found in the whole of the long catalogue of crime. You denied your guilt, and put yourself on your deliverance to the country. After a long, a patient, and an impartial trial, the country has decided against you, and most justly. You stand convicted of an aggravated breach of the great prohibition of the Almighty Creator of mankind, ' Thou shalt do no murder.' The law of this country, in concurrence with the law of all civilised countries, enforces this prohibition of God by exacting from the criminal who has violated it the forfeiture of his own life. And as this offence indicates the highest degree of cruelty to its unfortunate victim, and as it is dangerous to the peace, the order, and the security of society, justice assumes upon it her severest aspect, and allows no emotion of pity to shield the criminal from the punishment awarded to it both by the laws of God and by the laws of man. I advise you not to flatter yourself with any hopes of mercy upon earth. You sent this unfortunate woman to her account without giving her any time for preparation. She had no time to turn her eyes to the Throne of Grace for mercy and for forgiveness. She had no opportunity given to her to repent of her many transgressions: she had no time to throw herself on her knees and to implore for pardon at the Eternal Throne. The same measure is not meted out to you: a small interval is allowed you for preparation. Use it well, for the scene of this world closes upon you; but another and, I hope, a better world is opening for you. Remember the lessons of religion which you received in the early years of your childhood: consider the effects that may be produced by a sincere repentance—listen to the advice of the ministers of your religion, who will, I trust, console and advise you how best to meet the sharp ordeal which you must presently undergo. Nothing remains for me now to do, but to pass upon you the awful sentence of the law. That sentence is, that you be taken back to the prison from which you came, and that you be taken thence, on Monday next, to the place of execution, and there be hanged by the neck till you are dead, and that your body shall afterwards be dissected and anatomised; and the Lord God Almighty have mercy on your soul!"

The Lord Chief Baron, who was evidently much affected, then retired from the Court.

DEMEANOUR OF THE PRISONER DURING THE SUMMING UP OF THE LEARNED JUDGE, AND THE SENTENCE.

The prisoner paid the most eager attention to the earlier part of the summing up, in which his Lordship stated the indictment, and the necessity the law has imposed, of proving, to the satisfaction of the jury, that the death of the person has been occasioned by one of the means laid in the indictment: but when the Chief Baron told the jury that if they were satisfied that the death arose from any one, two, or more of the wounds inflicted on the body, and that those wounds were inflicted by the prisoner, they should find him guilty, his countenance fell, and he was apparently for some time in a state of stupor. He repeatedly bowed during the time the judge besought the jury to forget all the rumours and reports they had heard, and not to allow themselves to be influenced by the atrocious fact, if true, of a clergyman having preached to 5,000 persons in the immediate neighbourhood of the scene, a sermon, in which the prisoner was treated as the murderer. The Chief Baron's observations respecting the probable motive of the prisoner in enticing the deceased from her mother's house under the false statement that the constable had a warrant against her for a bastard child, made the strongest impression on the prisoner, whose countenance underwent several changes during the time. At one period, during the statement of the extraordinary conversation of Corder with Mrs. Stow, as to the number of children Maria had, the prisoner appeared almost in a fainting state, a transient paleness was visible in his countenance, his eyes rolled rapidly in their sockets, he heaved very deep sighs, and laid his head on the bar against which he had been previously leaning. From first to last, however, it was observed that he never shed a tear; but this may of course be attributed to his anxious attention to the investigation. One of the witnesses called by the prisoner, Mrs. Havers, a very pretty young woman, was frequently in tears during the detail of the evidence. He seemed to think the learned Judge would dwell at length upon his defence, and prepared himself, by a vigorous effort, to attend to the remarks he expected to hear on the subject. When, however, the Chief Baron passed over his story, by a bare statement of its principal points, and made not a single remark on it, but proceeded to read the evidence of his own witnesses, he relapsed into his former state of stupor and faintness, and so continued till the end of the charge. On the jury retiring to consider of his fate, he sat down on the bar in the dock, and leant his head against the beam on which he had previously rested his back. As the jurymen passed him, he cast upon each a piercing glance of the most intense interest. During the time of their absence, nothing could be more disconsolate and desponding than his appearance. On the jury returning into court, he once more resumed his standing position. On hearing the Foreman pronounce the fatal word "guilty," he raised his hand slowly to his forehead, pressed it for a moment, and then dropped it most dejectedly. His head immediately afterwards fell drooping upon his bosom. During the passing of the sentence, his firmness still continued in some degree, but at the close of it, he would have sunk to the ground, had he not been prevented by the compassionate attention of the governor of the gaol. He then sobbed loudly and convulsively for some moments, and was almost carried out of court by Mr. Orridge, and one of his attendants. Indeed, it was evident to all, that at this moment his faculties, both mental and bodily, were completely paralyzed. It was said that immediately after he quitted the dock, he fainted away; but we were given to understand that this was not the case. Shortly afterwards he was seen in the lock-up near to the court, with his head buried in his hands, which rested on his knees, and labouring under extreme emotion. After the court was cleared, he was removed to the county gaol.

The culprit, on his removal from Court, made a great effort to rally, even after the palpable extinction of his self-possession at the breaking up of the court—so much so, indeed, that even some of those about his person imagined his emotion had been assumed, for the purpose of exciting a sympathy from superficial observers, which even he, degraded as he was, must have known would be denied to him by every well-constituted mind. The Governor of the prison (who is represented to be a humane and considerate man) led him, first upon his return as a condemned criminal, into his private apartment, where he (probably fresh with the recollection of the suicide of a recent convict) p ainly, but mildly, informed the prisoner, he must forthwith exchange the whole of his apparel, because his (the governor's) situation with reference to him, had now become one of great responsibility, and he had a serious duty to discharge, which however he was ready to perform with every attention to the rational wants of a prisoner, in his awful situation. Corder immediately exchanged his clothes for those which were supplied to him from the prison stock, having previously given to his solicitor from his pocket his written defence, and some other papers. His penknife the governor took charge of, and a gentleman present remarked to Corder, that the evidence against him was too conclusive to be parried by any external appearances of evasion, and that it was due to his family and society to deliver his mind of the facts. To this provident suggestion the criminal gave no reply, and the only desire he expressed was to be allowed the society of his wife, who has been for a short time in lodgings in the town. The governor repeated to him that he should have every consolation which his situation and the rules of the prison permitted ; but that henceforth he could see nobody except in his presence or that of one of his officers, and that his own clothes should be at his disposal in exchange for those which he was at present under the necessity of substituting for them, on the day when he was to be brought out to die. At four o'clock Corder received some dinner from the governor's table, and a clergyman was sent for to afford him the solace (should he prove susceptible of it) of spiritual consolation.

When some allusion was made to the impropriety of allowing him to retain his pen-knife, (which, however, the Governor took from him yesterday), he said there was no danger to be apprehended in that respect, for he had no desire to add one sin to another. This was the only tendency towards any thing like confession which the prisoner disclosed yesterday evening. Two inmates of the prison, who are represented as being of serious and prudent characters, are to remain in Corder's cell until the time of his execution. A passage is preparing through the wall immediately adjoining the cell to the open paddock behind the gaol, where execution will be done upon the prisoner at 12 o'clock on Monday.

* * *

Publisher's note:

Inconsistencies in density, size and legibility of the above printed passages are regretted but, although enlarged from the original, are as faithfully reproduced as possible.

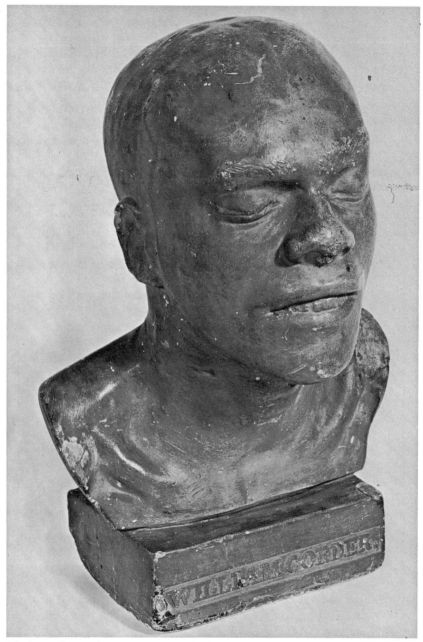

The bust of a simple country squire who has become as famous as many a monarch in history - perhaps even more famous than some . . .

Our other titles include:

MANY A SUMMER
Peter Hardiman Scott   ISBN 0 948134 32 1
Set in rural Suffolk at the turn of the century, the book gives a
warm insight into the life of a simple farmworker, told in the
colloquialisms of the main character, George Everett, and Hardiman
Scott's own inimitable style. There is also a moving account of
George's personal experiences on the Somme during the First
World War.

FACES WITH VOICES
June Freeman & Janine Wiedel   ISBN 0 948134 33 X
Against the backdrop of a small 20th century English market
town the book presents a set of contemporary life stories with
matching portraits by New Yorker Janine Wiedel. The text is rich
with the rhythms and inflections of the spoken voice and the
portraits have the relaxed informality which characterises docu-
mentary photography, resulting in an account of everyday lives
covering a broad spectrum of people. Foreward by Ronald
Blythe.

A LIVING IN THE PAST
David Hill   ISBN 0 948134 22 4
David Hill tells the story of his venture into the antique trade
following the purchase of an old forge in the heart of Suffolk. As
is his style, he often goes off at a tangent to talk about his life and
describes local crafts and customs. An absorbing read whether or
not your interest lies in antiques.

ROSES IN A SUFFOLK GARDEN
Josephine Walpole   ISBN 0 948134 24 0
Despite its parochial title, this is a book dedicated to the traditional English Rose. The author lives in Suffolk and writes with
feeling of the roses that fill her country garden. Beautifully
illustrated with water colour paintings by Anne Rea, the book is
introduced and recommended by that authority on the rose, Jack
Harkness, O.B.E.

RICHARD CASTELL PUBLISHING LIMITED